MW00711235

THE

COMPLETE

CABINET MAKER,

AND

UPHOLSTERER'S GUIDE

BY

J. STOKES

1829

The Toolemera Press
History Preserved

www.toolemera.com

THE COMPLETE CABINET MAKER AND
UPHOLSTERER'S GUIDE
by J. Stokes
Dean & Munday, Threadneedle Street, London
1829

International Standard Book Number
ISBN : 978-0-9831500-6-0
Hard Cover

Published by
The Toolemera Press
Massachusetts, U.S.A.

www.toolemera.com

Manufactured in the United States of America

Introduction to the Toolemera edition of *The Complete Cabinet Maker And Upholsterer's Guide*.

The facsimile reprint of the first edition, from 1829, of *The Complete Cabinet Maker And Upholsterer's Guide* by J. Stokes (Stokes) has been produced to encompass as many of the original visual details as possible.

Each page has been carefully reproduced at original size, retaining the color and textural details inherent in a 184 year old book. Cleansing was limited to surface removal of loose dirt. Finger marks and other indications of age and usage were left intact in keeping with the historic role this book played as a major reference resource to the skilled trades of the nineteenth and early twentieth centuries.

In reading Stokes, you will note that each page is held within a .75 inch white border. The digital printing process requires a clear border between the page edge and any text and images. Framing the page image in this fashion precludes the risk of original page elements being cut off at the inner margin as well as the outer, top or bottom edges.

It is our goal to provide for our readers the experience of owning and enjoying a rare book. We hope you enjoy the read.

Who was J. Stokes and how did *The Complete Cabinet Maker And Upholsterer's Guide* become the standard reference for nearly a century?

As of the publishing of the Toolemera edition, there has been no new evidence as to who J. Stokes was, what his or her first name was or from whence Stokes came. The name J. Stokes appears on the first and fourth editions, 1829 and 1841, respectively, both published by Dean & Munday, Threadneedle Street, London. Beginning in 1850, Henry Carey Baird & Co. of Philadelphia, Pennsylvania, United States of America, began publication once again under the authorship of J. Stokes and continued to publish with this name through to their final edition of 1904.

How Stokes came to traverse the Atlantic Ocean requires an association between an early British publisher and a famous early American publishing empire.

The story begins with The Minerva Printing Press, founded in the late eighteenth century by Mr. Lane of Cree Church Lane, Leadenhall Street, London. Mr. Lane subsequently formed a partnership with Mr. A. K. Newman, another British publisher of the period. Minerva Press specialized in light novels of a gothic nature, which titles today we term Romance Novels and latter in children's literature.

In the introduction to *Dame Wiggins Of Lee And Her Seven Wonderful Cats* by Mrs. Richard Scranton Sharpe Pearson, published by Dean & Son in 1860 and re-published in 1887 by Field & Tuer, Tuer notes that Newman "... occasionally re-published an American book, Carey and Lee (sic), of Philadelphia, usually acting as his agents." Therein lies the connection between the London editions of Stokes and the Philadelphia editions.

The Carey publishing family tree included M. Carey & Sons, Carey & Lea, Lea & Blanchard, Carey & Hart and eventually, Henry Carey Baird & Co., all of Philadelphia. Henry Carey Baird & Co., organized in 1849, was the first American publisher to specialize in books of a technical and industrial nature. Thus we have the connection between London and Philadelphia for Stokes.

Although it remains a mystery as to why Dean & Munday initially chose to publish a technical title amidst their book list of novels and children's offerings, the clear success of Stokes through four editions speaks for their maintaining it in their catalog. The literary friendship between Newman and the Carey publishing family must have been close enough for Baird to purchase the rights to publish Stokes in America.

In considering the London market, the popularity and familiarity of the Minerva Press / Dean & Munday / A. K. Newman publishing imprints must have served to provide a stepping stone for a possibly unknown author. Publishers were often printers as well as book sellers, thus on display in their windows and on their shelfs could be found a wide variety of titles in both bound and unbound forms. The buyer usually had the option of choosing the type of binding according to the depth of their pocket.

On record for Stokes is a paper on card covered edition featuring a blue paper printed with most of the original title page. From this I would surmise a ready-for-sale edition to be displayed in a sales window or on a shelf. I have also seen period full leather bound and period quarter leather with marbled paper bound editions which appear to have been ordered by the buyer.

The Painter, Gilder, And Varnisher's Companion, also published by H. C. Baird & Co., in 1850, and *The Complete Cabinet Maker And Upholsterer's Guide*, retitled *The Complete Cabinet Maker And Upholsterer's Companion* for the American market, were both deemed of sufficient importance by Baird & Co. to be offered in their inaugural book list. Each book was in continuous publication from 1850 through the early part of the 20th century

The Painter, Gilder, And Varnisher's Companion, 1850, edited by Henry Carey Baird, is offered by Toolemera as part of it's classic reprint series.

There were, at the very least, two books of the period with similar titles: Hepplewhite's *The Cabinet-Maker And Upholsterer's Guide*, 1788 and George Smith's *Cabinet-Maker & Upholsterer's Guide*, 1826. Both are primarily pattern books, a form of book that offered furniture designs and often instructions in geometry, perspective, and ornamental drawing as well as various finishing receipts (compilations of materials, instructions, 'secret' formula, etc.). Pattern books were frequently used as marketing tools by the craftsman during discussions with a customer over a proposed project.

In comparing pattern books of the period to Stokes, the differences are evident. Stokes provides introductions to geometry and perspective by way of glossaries and brief explanations of processes. Design and fashion are addressed minimally and, notably, unchanged in description from the first edition of 1829 through to the last of 1904. The only substantive changes in Stokes are the addition of an appendix on French Polishing in 1880 and the exclusion of the eleven hand colored plates of furniture designs after the 1829 edition.

The bulk of Stokes contains receipts for the compounding and application of finishing materials, descriptions of various forms of cabinetwork and upholstery, how to clean and maintain both shop tools and completed furniture, &c., &c.. Stokes was therefore, a reference book for the daily operations of a workshop rather than a pattern book to be used in the preparation of an order from a prospective customer.

The question of plagiarism is often raised when discussing early books. The modern views and legal terms of copyright did not exist at the time of Stokes. It was common practice for authors of pattern books, as well as books of receipts, to liberally borrow from both current and past writings. While there was some small recourse if an author wished to pursue a case of plagiarism in civil court, very few did so.

More Reprints From Toolemera

- Mechanick Exercises, 1703 by Joseph Moxon

- The Mechanic's Companion, 1850 by Peter Nicholson

- The Circle Of The Mechanical Arts, 1813 by Thomas Martin

- Wood Carving, 1896 by Joseph Phillips

- Woodwork Tools And How To Use Them, 1922 by William Fairham

- Woodwork Joints, 1920 by William Fairham

- Cabinet Construction, 1930 by J. C. S. Brough

- Furniture Making: Advanced Projects In Woodwork, 1912 by Ira Griffith

- The Painter, Gilder, And Varnisher's Companion, 1850 Edited by Henry Carey Baird

- Our Workshop, 1866 by Temple Thorold

- Carpentry And Joinery For Amateurs, 1879 by James Lukin

- The Art Of Mitring, 1892 by Owen Maginnis

- Working Drawings Of Colonial Furniture, 1912, F. J. Bryant

www.shop.toolemera.com

THE
COMPLETE CABINET MAKER,
AND UPHOLSTERER'S GUIDE :
COMPRISING,
THE RUDIMENTS AND PRINCIPLES
OF
CABINET-MAKING AND UPHOLSTERY,
WITH
FAMILIAR INSTRUCTIONS, ILLUSTRATIONS BY EXAMPLES,
FOR ATTAINING A PROFICIENCY IN
THE ART OF DRAWING :
THE PROCESSES OF VENEERING, INLAYING, AND BUHL-WORK :
THE
ART OF DYING AND STAINING WOOD WORK,
BONE, TORTOISESHELL, &c.
DIRECTIONS FOR LACKERING, JAPANNING, AND VARNISHING :
TO MAKE FRENCH POLISH ;
TO PREPARE THE BEST GLUES, CEMENTS, & COMPOSITIONS ;
AND
A NUMBER OF RECEIPTS,
PARTICULARLY USEFUL TO THE WORKMEN GENERALLY.

EMBELLISHED WITH
SIXTEEN EXPLANATORY AND ILLUSTRATIVE ENGRAVINGS,
BY
Mr. J. STOKES,
With the Articles of Furniture elegantly coloured.

London;
PUBLISHED BY DEAN & MUNDAY, THREADNEEDLE STREET.

Drapery for Three Windows.

INTRODUCTORY OBSERVATIONS.

The very great improvement to which the arts and manufactures of this country have attained, within the last fifty years, renders it essential that every person engaged therein should use his utmost endeavours to obtain a perfect knowledge of the trade or art which he professes to follow. —The workmen of the last century were, comparatively speaking, but with few exceptions, mechanical beings, who worked by rule, unguided by any scientific principles, and followed step by step the beaten track of their ancestors: the workmen of the present day have the road of science opened for them; the clue of knowledge is unwound to the enquiring mind; but unless industry and perseverence accompany them in the pursuit of information, they will never obtain sufficient to justify a pretension even to a mediocre knowledge of the principles of their respective arts.

These remarks apply to scientific and mechanical professions generally; but to the cabinet-

A 3

maker and upholsterer they attach with peculiar
force.—It is not enough for a person following
either of these branches of domestic decoration
to have attained the character of a *good workman*,
that being now considered a mere negative
phrase, implying only that quantum of excel-
lence which consists in following implicitly the
directions of others; or imitating with neatness
and accuracy their details and plans. In a business where change and caprice rule with un-
bounded sway,—in which the fashion of to-day
may become obselete to-morrow, and in which
novelty forms the greatest recommendation,—an
inventive genius and discriminating judgment
are, certainly, essential qualifications; and if
the young workman ever feels the least ambition
to excel, or entertains a wish to rise above the
bench, he will find them to be not only essential,
but actually indispensible.

In this business, as well as in many others,
the workman who understands the principles of
his trade, and applies them correctly in practice,
has a decided advantage over his fellow-work-
men; and if to his superior knowledge he add a
steadiness of manner, and industrious habits,
his endeavours cannot fail to secure approbation,

while his worth will be certainly and duly appreciated.

If, then, in order to secure constant employment—the only means of ensuring comfort to himself and family—it is essential that the *workman* should excel, how much more must it behove the person who *superintends* a business of the kind, to be fully acquainted with every department of the business: for how can any one pretend to direct others, who is himself in need of information? Nor is this all; it will often fall to his province to sketch out new designs, or to alter or improve those in present use: if his employer or a respectable customer should not approve of the fashion or ornamental embellishment of any new article of furniture submitted to their approbation, a superintendant would feel himself sadly at a loss, if he could neither sketch out the improvements or alterations which his own genius might suggest, nor embody those pointed out by others.

Again; the researches of the chemist are daily adding to a stock of information valuable to every department of the arts and sciences; among these the cabinet-maker and upholsterer will find many peculiarly serviceable—witness the modern improvements in cements, varnishes, gilding, polishing, and every other part of ornamental decoration. The experience of few indeed is sufficiently extensive to enable them to store their minds with one tenth part of the infromation which has been published to the world on these heads. A work, therefore, which contains the most approved receipts,—and from which the workman will be enabled to select those applicable to his purpose,—will be appreciated as equally useful and necessary.

This work, now submitted to the public under the title of THE CABINET-MAKER, AND UPHOLSTERERS' GUIDE, is intended as a book of useful information to the apprentice, a work of real utility to the workman, and a manual of experimental reference to the trade generally: it does not profess to give diffuse instructions how to make a table, a chair, or any similar article of furniture: that would be not only superfluous and unnecessary, but a vain attempt: practice only—and that under good instruction—can make a good workman or a neat finisher: our aim has been to produce a work which shall give those instructions which are not always to be met with in every one's practice, but which are not the less essential to be known by every workman.

To make our work useful, and easy of reference, we have adopted the popular plan of dividing the subjects into distinct parts, and of again subdividing them under their proper heads. This will enable any one to trace out any particular direction or receipt with facility, and shew, generally at one view, all we have to say upon the subject.

Part I comprises the rudiments and principles of ornamental cabinet-making and upholstery generally; and contains plain and familiar instructions, exemplified by easy examples, for attaining a proficiency in the art of drawing, particularly that department applicable to the cabinet-maker and upholsterer. In this part we have endeavoured to lead the student step by step from first principles to the more determinate forms; and, by placing before his views the progressive examples, to render the attainment of this useful art equally speedy and certain.

We have not only endeavoured, in this part,

to practise the pupil in such a familiar and progressive manner as to render it a pleasing recreation rather than abstract study; but we have also laid down the most approved principles for the developement and exercise of his inventive faculties, in the practise of the ornamental department of his art, and to lay before him such elegant and classic designs, and such modern examples of furniture, as will lead him instinctively to form a style at once chaste and appropriate.

Part II comprises the processes of veneering, inlaying, and finishing in buhl-work, the ornamental decorations used in cabinet-work.—In this part, such directions are given as experience has warranted to be most certain of properly and successfully performing the embellishment in a neat and complete manner; the materials best adapted for the purpose, are also pointed out; and the cements and glues most suited for this kind of work, described.

Part III comprises dying and staining woods, ivory, bone, tortoiseshell, musical instruments, and all other manufactured articles; with the processes of silvering, gilding, and bronzing.—

In this we have laid down the most approved directions for the selection of the wood or other article best adapted for the required process; the method of preparing it, and the dye or stain best calculated to give it the desired colour; and in the silvering, gilding, and bronzing, nothing has been omitted which modern improvement has added to realize these branches in the highest style of brilliancy.

Part IV comprises lackering, japanning, varnishing, and polishing every article of cabinet and upholstery work; and contains all the improved processes practised in each of their departments, including India-japanning and the French polishing; together with plain directions for making and employing the best and most brilliant lackers, japans, and varnishes, according to the receipts of the most celebrated manufacturers.

Part V contains glues, cements, and compositions for filling-up and ornamenting articles of furniture; and a considerable number of miscellaneous receipts—the result of experience, or selected from the writings of the most approved authors, and the more scientific works.

Such is the outline of its contents: as to its merits, we submit our opinion to the test of a discerning public, in the confident expectation that the Complete Cabinet-maker and Upholsterer's Guide will soon find a place in every factory and workshop, and be the companion of every intelligent workman.

London, June 1829.

COMPLETE CABINET-MAKER,

AND

UPHOLSTERERS' GUIDE.

———

PART I.

ORNAMENTAL CABINET-MAKING:

CONTAINING, THE RUDIMENTS OF DRAWING, AS APPLI-
CABLE TO ARTICLES OF FURNITURE;—PRIMARY OB-
SERVATIONS ON DRAWING ORNAMENTS FOR CABINET-
WORK;—GEOMETRICAL AND PERSPECTIVE TERMS DE-
FINED AND EXPLAINED;—THE RUDIMENTS OF SHA-
DOWING, AND OF COLOURING;—ORNAMENTS USED IN
CABINET-WORK, THEIR TERMS EXPLAINED;—ORNA-
MENTAL DECORATIONS, WHERE AND WHEN MOST
APPLICABLE.

———

THE RUDIMENTS OF DRAWING,
as applicable to Articles of Furniture.

DRAWING is the art of delineating on an appropriate
surface the representions of objects, as they appear to
the eye, or are formed by the inventive powers of a correct taste. It takes in a wide range, but the parts
more intimately connected with cabinet-work, are—
Geometry, and Perspective.

B

Geometrical drawing may be defined to be that branch which delineates any given object according to certain fixed forms or proportions, and represents the whole subject apportioned by a given scale; perspective, on the contrary, represents it in the same manner as the eye actually beholds the given figure, the fore parts being most conspicuous, while those distant appear more indistinct, or rather as if they receded from the sight.

The preparatory studies consist in various modes of delineating by light and dark strokes; the more mature operations of the art are—shadowing, and colouring.

Drawing of this description may be divided into outline and shading: the outline, or contour, represents the boundaries of an object, as they appear to terminate against the back-ground, and is a section of the whole mass. Outlines are also used for the circumscription of all the parts of an object, interior as well as exterior; while shading, with a softer pencil, expresses the projections, cavities, or flatness, which form its anterior features.

A correct outline of the objects of a picture, is of the highest importance, and, certainly, the best test of an intelligent daughtsman, as it in most cases conveys the general character of the object, without the aid of shading; and is therefore, as far as it goes, a complete drawing in itself. The aim of the student, therefore, should be, to acquire the power of copying faithfully whatever may present itself before him.

For the first essay, no material is better than a soft
pencil; the drawing to be sketched on white paper,
and the pencil to be held somewhat in the same manner as a pen, but so as to allow of more freedom of
action, and to give a greater facility of motion both to
the fingers and the wrist. The learner should begin
with making lines parallel, straight, and curved in all
directions, and then exercise himself in tracing geometrical figures, into some of which all forms may be re-
solved; but without, as yet, the aid of either rule or
compass : he should also copy occasionally from broad
specimens of ornament, as being well adapted to give
firmness and flexibility to the hand, to increase which
they should be practised upon as large a scale as convenient. He may also at intervals study from the best
drawings, or from open chalk prints.

Whatever be the object to be drawn, its general
form should be first sketched out very slightly, that
any fault may be the more easily removed; estimate,
as nearly as you can, the distances of particular points
in the original figure ; make dots at similar distances
on your paper; then draw your lines carefully to these
dots, beginning at the upper part, and working down-
ward, either from right to left, or from left to right,
according to the tendency of the parts: draw the principal divisions first; when these appear right, mark in
the smaller parts, and when the whole is pencilled out,
examine it scrupulously; then pass over it with a piece
of bread, to render the lines nearly invisible, and re-

vise and retouch them again and again, till the sketch
be correct: after this, go over the whole with a harder
pencil; or the lines may be put in ink with a sable
brush, first comparing all the parts with the original,
both perpendicularly and horizontally, that they may
have the same comparative inclination, range, and distance, as the object itself. Where the student is at a
loss, he may now sparingly use the compass or sector,
but only by way of proving the angles after he has
done his utmost; for unless these instruments be oftener
used in the eye than in the hand of the learner, he will
never make a good draughtsman, or be able to judge of
distance in any other way than by rule. Perhaps it
would be best for learners to make their first lessons as
near the size of the originals as possible; and when the
eye can measure with tolerable exactness, to vary from
these dimensions will be proper; the pupil will then
acquire an aptness of preserving similar proportions on
a different scale, which forms so essential a part of the
draughtsman's skill, and is so indispensible in imitating
objects or drawings. It is not necessary that the lines
in a drawing should be of one uniform thickness; on
the contrary, a delicate variety, with the lines occasionally broken, gives a richness and adds much to the
effect: the lines may also be carried a little within the
contour of the hollows, as if pursuing the inflection of
the part, which, when done with skill, makes a mere
outline very characteristic.

    These remarks apply to Drawing generally; we shall

now give a few primary observations regarding the principles of the art, as applied to cabinet and upholstery work.

ON DRAWING ORNAMENTS

For Cabinet-Work.

IT will be to little purpose that the young workman should possess a correct discrimination in the choice of the most appropriate ornaments, if he have not some knowledge of drawing; for without he can delineate the embellishment in outline, he will never be enabled to execute it in the wood. For this purpose, his first acquirement must be, to trace an object by the eye, in all its relative proportions and inclinations, with a just boldness and freedom of hand. To facilitate this, his best way will be to begin by drawing the most simple forms, as straight lines; and proceed gradually to the more complex objects; but whatever subject be his first essay, he must place it perpendicularly and directly before him, otherwise he will never produce a correct drawing. He must also bear in mind while he is copying, what are the details of the object, as well as what is merely before him; otherwise, he will never learn to delineate with correctness.

From straight lines, he should next proceed to curved and spiral ones of different descriptions, branching off to the right hand and to the left: in this he must be particular, although he will at first find it somewhat difficult to make his sides correspond.

After drawing lines in all the various directions his fancy can dictate, he will acquire a command of hand, and a ready facility of delineating in every possible position.

The best method of learning, generally, is for the pupil to draw a few simple parallel lines, and after this, to copy curved lines, and then to multiply them to the number of ten or more: these being done, he may try leaves and scrolls; and, lastly, the whole ramifications of foliage.

We will illustrate this part of our introductory instruction, with several lessons, by way of examples, *See plates* 2 *and* 3.

Plate 2.—*Lesson* 1. Various simple lines for the pupil's first practice.

Plate 3,—*Lesson* 2. Simple and compound lines and forms; with a figure (10) in outline, half-shade, and full shade.

These preliminary lessons should be well practised before the pupil proceeds further onwards; for however simple they may seem, they are as necessary and important a part of drawing, as the foundation-stone is to the building; they are indeed the very laws of the art; and it is by a tasteful combination of these forms that

the most correct pictures and the most accurate deli-
neations are produced.

Having practised thus far, the student may next
attempt the combinations, or compound forms, as ter-
minal ornaments, vases, pedestals, columns, leaves,
scrolls, and similar embellishments; of these we shall
give a few lessons, but which, in the hand of a judicious
student, will be amply sufficient. *See plates* 4 *and* 5.

Plate 4.—*Lesson* 3. Various compound ornaments
and scrolls, in outline and shade, peculiarly suitable
for cabinet work, and well adapted as practical lessons
to the pupil.

Plate 5.—*Lesson* 4. Compound ornaments, continued.

When the student has copied these over several
times, and attained sufficient practice in copying from
drawings with precision, and can measure distances
with the eye, and delineate them with a free hand,
he should then try at drawing from plaster casts; after
which he may practice from the vegetable creation
such plants and flowers as are best calculated for his
future purpose. By proceeding thus, he will soon become a proficient; he may therefore now try the fertility
of his own powers, by applying himself to the com-
posing of ornaments, which will rarely fail to appear
graceful, rich, and natural.

In designing ornaments, the pupil must picture the
whole subject in his imagination, as though dazzling on
the paper before him; he should then, with a black-lead

pencil, mark it out faintly in lightly sketched lines ; which having completed, he may lower the whole with crumbs of bread, and lastly retrace it more correctly. The ornament may now be inked in with a pen, or with a fine sable-hair brush, or worked up in pencil, as the artist may consider best.

GEOMETRICAL AND PERSPECTIVE TERMS

Defined and Explained.

WE have said that the parts of drawing more intimately connected with our subject, are, Geometry, and Perspective. It will therefore be necessary that the terms in common use be defined; as without a knowledge of them, it will be almost impossible to understand many of the directions essential to the cabinet-maker or upholsterer.

GEOMETRY.

Extension is a term applied to any expanded surface, proceeding in any or every direction.

Magnitude is a solid bulk, having length, breadth, and thickness.

A *Figure* is any bounded space: when formed of a plain surface, it is termed a *plain* figure.

A *superficial* figure has length and breadth only.

A *solid* figure has length, breadth, and thickness.

Surfaces are the extremities of solids.

Lines are the confines of *surfaces*.

Points are the terminations or intersections of lines.

Angles are the concentration or conjunction of two inclined lines; and are either right, acute, or obtuse.

A *curve* is that kind of line from which if two points be taken, the intercepted point is not straight.

A *quadrangle* is a plain square figure bounded by four right lines.

A *parallelogram* is an oblong quadrangle, the opposite sides of which are perfectly parallel.

A *quadrilateral* is a quadrangle formed by four equal lines.

A *rhombus* is a quadrangle, having its sides equal, and its angles two equally obtuse, and two equally acute.

A *rhomboid* is an oblique-angled parallelogram, whose opposite sides and angles are equal to each other.

A *trapezium* is a figure with none of its sides parallel.

A *trapeziod* hath two only of its opposite sides parallel.

All plain figures having more than four sides, are termed *polygons*; and are named from the number of sides they contain; five sides, a *pentagon*; six, a *hexagon*; seven, a *heptagon*; eight, an *octagon*; &c.

A *circle* is formed by an uniform curved line, called its *circumference*; which curve is in every part equally distant from the point termed its *centre*.

A *triangle* is a figure having three equal sides.

A *semicircle* is half a circle.

A *segment of a circle* is more or less than half of a circle.

The *diameter of a circle* is a straight line drawn through its centre, each end joining to the circumference.

A *chord* is a right line drawn within a circle, its ends both joining the extremities of the arc.

The *radius of a circle* is a right line drawn from the centre to the circumference.

The construction or formation of most of these geometrical figures or parts, are so self-evident from their definition, that we need not give any delineation of their figure, but leave them for the student's exercise: in which, indeed, he can scarcely fail of correctness. We shall therefore now proceed to the

PERSPECTIVE.

If the student hold up at arm's-length a picture-frame, in which is a square or oblong piece of glass washed over with whitehard varnish, but perfectly dry, he will be enabled to delineate with a pencil the visible lineaments or outline appearance of the object as seen within the compass of the frame; which result will be the lineal picture, the glass being considered the paper on which the objects are to be drawn. The true relative proportions of perspective will be here laid down; and if after the design is sketched out, the whole is proportioned by a scale, it will greatly facilitate the student, particularly if he should afterwards wish to enlarge or decrease the size of his object. In this case a border may be drawn at equal or certain distances from the extremities of every part; and the whole space both in breadth and depth be apportioned into equal divisions and marked by pencil lines intersecting the whole and each other; and if on a smaller or larger paper, the same number of divisions be made, the student will have a guide which will hardly allow him to err in preserving the due and relative proportions in the copy as existed in the original. To illustrate this, see *plate 6, diag. 1.* The spectator is viewing the appearance which two pieces of furniture will have at a distance; when seen through a similar medium to the one just named, the result will be the same, and prove this position in perspective to be correct, viz. that all objects situated on a level floor, diminish, and seem to advance up or ascend the picture, in the same proposition as they recede from the sight; while those suspended from or on a level ceiling, have the appearance of *descending,* or seeming lower in the picture, in the same proportion according to their distance from the eye of the spectator.

Diagram 2, will show the terms made use of; for example, the figure represents a hall which is thrown into perspective; in this case A B are the base lines, C. D. the points of view or distance; the line which is drawn from the one to the other is the horizontal line, and E the point of sight. We have divided the base line into six equal parts, to show the dimension of each square, (for we will suppose the hall to be paved;) from each of these divisions draw lines to the point of sight, E; then draw diagonal lines from the extremities of your base line to the points of view, and where the visual lines are cut by the diagonal ones, draw parallel lines, and the diminution of each square will be given correctly. It will be easily seen we have determined the width of the door at two squares on the base, which carried to the point of distance, intersect the side wall, and gives the width against it; the thickness is likewise carried out on the base line, and carried to the points of sight E, and gives the depth of the door. Thus, by practising a few similar plans, the first rudiments of the art will be easily understood, and found both useful and amusing.

The following are the most common, and at the same time the most essential terms, used in Perspective.

The *point of view* is the optic angle of the visual rays, or point where the rays from the picture or object concentrate; and where the spectator is supposed to stand while drawing the object—it is consequently out of the picture, but is the point or distance from which only will the picture or object appear natural.

The *point of sight*, or more properly the *seat of the eye*, is a point in the picture directly opposite the eye, and is produced by a line drawn at right angles to the picture.

The *horizontal line* is a line passing before, and of the exact height of the eye of the spectator.

The *primitive object* is the figure given to be delineated.

Primitive measures are the real measures of the object reduced to a scale, which by being thrown obliquely into perspective, will be seen foreshortened.

The *base plane* is the floor or part on which the object is supposed to be situated.

The *base line*, or entering line, is that on which the transparent plane is supposed to be posited.

The *vanishing points* are those in the horizontal line to which all the oblique points concentrate or meet.

Inclined vanishing points are ascertained by perpendicular lines raised from the extreme vanishing point in the horizontal line; and are essential for pediments and swing glasses.

The *diagonal vanishing point* is a point set off upon the horizontal line either way from the *seat of the eye*; and in the same proportionate measure as the draughtsman is supposed to stand distant from the picture, or object.

THE RUDIMENTS OF SHADOWING.

WHEN the objects are correctly drawn in outline, the learner should proceed with shadowing, first laying on the dark broad washes, then the next in strength, and lastly the more delicate half-tints. In finishing, great attention must be paid to the quantities and com-

binations of light, middle tint, shadow, and reflec-
tion: in this, the young student will find some difficulty in distinguishing the delicate gradations of light
and shade; but observation and practice will soon
teach him. We may, however, remark, that he must
reserve his greatest strength of light and shade for the
parts most prominent, and every light must be accom-
panied and supported by its shade; the middle tint
becomes deeper in tone as it advances from the light,
till it is lost in the shadow, and the outline is softened
into the back-ground by reflections from the surrounding objects; the contour, therefore, must not be too
strongly marked, or the extreme parts, which should
retire, will come forward.

Shadows are made out by washing or tinting the
drawing with Indian ink, which should never be mixed
up for use a second time, after having once dried in the
saucer, or it will work muddy. A neutral tint, made
with Venitian red and indigo, or lamp-black, burnt
terra de sienna, and lake, varied as circumstances and
distance may require, may also be used for this purpose.

Shading may be performed on columns or other
convex bodies in two different ways: the first is, that
of laying on the shades, as nearly in their places as
possible, with a tint very nearly dark enough, then
softening off the edges with a clean brush with water,
and, when dry, repeating the process several times
until sufficiently lightened: the other is, by working

with tints rather lighter than are requisite, at first laid in spots near each other, and then blended by a faint wash over the whole, and when nearly dry, strengthened by other spots in the interstices, and so on, gradually giving the shades their due force and form, leaving the paper for the lights. This mode is called *stippling*, and in the hands of a master, is the best, or at least the boldest, for finished drawings; for it not only occasions the whole picture to sparkle, but gives a transparency and play to the shadows, making, as it were, darkness visible. It is, however, of little importance which of these, or any other plan of shading, be adopted, so that the faithfulness of the imitation be well attended to.

In the representations of shadows, the artist should be careful not to make them too hard or abrupt at the edges, because every shadow terminates by the faint and indistinct transition from the obscure to the illuminated part of the surface upon which such shadows are cast. Nor should shadows be equally dark; for it is to be remembered that shadows projected by the sun are softened by the surrounding rays and by the general diffusion of light through the atmosphere; they should, therefore, be darkest near the object that produces them. It is on this principle that shadows from the light of a candle, are darker than those from the sun; although the light is much more forcible from the latter body: hence it follows, that shadows in candlelight scenes must,

in the language of painting, be heavier in their representation, or less transparent, than those of daylight.

For examples of shadowing, see fig. 10, plate 3, and
plates 4 and 5.

THE RUDIMENTS OF COLOURING.

A JUDICIOUS writer has observed, that "Should the
most skilful master draw a rose or grape with the
pencil only, his observers would have but a faint
or imperfect image of the object; but let him add to
each its proper colours, and we no longer doubt—we
smell the rose, we touch the grape." Colouring
may therefore be considered as the life and soul of a
picture: it is the third and last component—that of
giving to objects their proper hue and colour, as they
appear under all the combinations of light, middle
tint, and shadow; and also of blending and contrasting
them, so as to make each appear with the greatest
brilliancy and advantage.

Colouring may be divided into two kinds: that
which is necessary for rendering the imitation just
and natural; and that which is fascinating, and renders
the work more impressive on the imagination—more
delightful to the eye. Truth alone in the local tints
is required in the first: the second demands choice in
their selection; for the eye has the same intuitive
abhorrence of unharmonious combinations of colour,
that the ear has to discordant sounds. To possess a

scientific knowledge of the arrangement of colours, so as to produce effects not unnatural, requires but little talent; but to perform all that a skilful combination and application of the various powers of colours can effect, is not so easily attained.

As, however, the student may by this time have attained a sufficient knowledge of drawing to be able to pourtray any subject he sees, his fancy may invent, or his employer suggest, he will now only require a few hints as to the colours that may be compounded with the best effect for imitating in drawings the different woods, metals, cloths, &c. used in the various articles of cabinet furniture, stating the principal colours first.

To imitate mahogany.—Mix light red with burnt umber; shadow with burnt umber.

Rose-wood.—Mix lake and lamp black; shadow with a stronger tint of the same while wet.

Satin-wood.—Use yellow ochre; shadow with Vandyke brown.

Bronze.—Mix Prussian-blue, gamboge, and burnt-umber; shadow with Vandyke brown and indigo, mixed.

Brass.—Use gamboge; shadow with burnt terra de sienna, and stipple with burnt-umber: *inlaid brass* or *buhl ornaments* may be laid on afterwards with a body colour made of gamboge and whiting.

Or-moulu.—Mix king's yellow and Indian yellow.

Velvet.—Mix carmine and Indian red.

Green-baize.—Mix indigo and gamboge:—for chair-seats, use vermillion.

Glass.—Mix lamp-black and indigo; shadow with the same.

Porphry-marble.—Mix lake, Venitian red, and ivory-black; afterwards speckle with constant-white, and with lamp-black.

Verd-antique.—Mix indigo and Roman-ochre; afterwards lay on light and dark green spots.

Sienna-marble.—Mix raw terra de sienna and burnt-umber; vein it with burnt umber alone.

Mona-marble.—Mix indigo, Venitian red, and lake; vein with dark green.

Black-marble.—Mix indigo and madder-brown with lamp-black.

Buff-colour drapery.—Mix gamboge and Roman ochre, or gamboge and a little lake; shadow with the same, darker; for the more intense shadows, mix gamboge and burnt-umber.

White drapery.—Shade with a mixture of Indian ink and indigo.

Chintz.—Shadow with a mixture of lake and gamboge.

Crimson-curtains.—Colour with red lead and a little lake.

Gilt-poles.—Colour as for *or-moulu*, and shadow with burnt-umber and gamboge combined, or with burnt-umber and lake, and sometimes with a mixture of lake and gamboge.

There is scarcely an artist but who compounds

colours each in a manner peculiar to himself; now, as landscapes are sometimes seen through the apertures of windows, when a view of the room is taken, some instruction is necessary in this department of the art; we shall therefore state what is considered to be the best and simplest process.

After the view is penciled out, begin with the *sky:* for this use a mixture of Prussian-blue and a little lake; begin at the top of the picture, and soften it downwards, but at the horizon add a little Venitian red. The *clouds* are next to be worked in with a mixture of Venitian red, indigo, and a little gamboge; next, with the sky-colour, and a little Venitian red added, cover the whole of the *ground*, beginning at the front, and thinning it towards the horizon; but observe not to go over the *rivers*, or pieces of *water*. *Distant mountains* are coloured with indigo and lake ; *near, fuscous mountains*, with indigo, lake, and burnt terra de sienna : *distant parts* of the *grass*, are made with indigo, yellow-ochre, and lake; *near grass* is made with burnt sienna, Italian pink, and indigo: *dark touches* on the *fore-ground* are of Vandyke brown, indigo, and burnt terra de sienna; *intense dark touches*, of lamp-black and burnt-umber; *distant trees*, are worked with indigo, lake, and gamboge, shadowed with the same colour made darker; and *near trees* are coloured with burnt sienna, gamboge, and indigo, deepened towards the shadowed side. This is all that is required to be known in this branch of the art; and is a complete and valuable, though concise, process for painting cabinet furniture, landscapes, &c.

ORNAMENTS USED IN CABINET-WORK,

THEIR TERMS EXPLAINED.

ORNAMENTS are the decorative parts of an edifice, household furniture, or other objects, studied from the vegetable and animal kingdoms, gracefully and artificially combined. They are seldom of importance on the exteriors of buildings, simplicity and variety in the contour, with bold, massive forms, being there primarily considered, and on which their grandeur chiefly depends : it is in the interior that ornaments should be principally applied, where they are not liable to be destroyed by the weather, and are likewise brought nearer to the eye of the beholder.

Foliage ornament is composed of leaves only; the subdivisions of a leaf are called *plants ;* and the small, external divisions, *raffles ;* the terminations of the plants are called *eyes*, and the longer reeds proceeding from the eyes are called *pipes*. The leaves chiefly used, are the acanthus, olive, palm, parsley, vine, ivy, oak, thistle, laurel, lotus, and water leaf; the flowers most in use are, the honey-suckle, lotus, lily, rose, and jasmine.

Mixed ornament is a composition of leaves, fruit, flowers, and scrolls, combined in any way with each other.

Festooned ornament is comprised of fruit, flowers, and leaves, intermixed with each other, and supported at the two extremities with ribands, sometimes suspended from a bull's-horns, the middle part formed with a parabolic curve by its gravity.

Arabesque ornament is a mixture of slender scrolls, leaves, vases, birds, lyres, and representations of human figures.

Winding-foliage has a principal plant from which issues a stem in the form of a serpentine line, with a number of branches spreading out on each side of all the convex parts of the alternate sides, and twisting themselves in the form of spiral lines; and those spirals and stalks are decorated with foliage and flowerets.

Serpentined or running ornament has a trunk, from which springs a stem continually changing its course in opposite directions, that is, first concave, then convex, and so on alternately to any multiplied number of curves of contrary natures; from the concave and convex parts shoot branches, each terminating with a rose.

Plaited ornament is a definite number of serpentine lines, interwoven with each other; and exclusively in the cap of the Grecian Ionic order.

Guilloche ornament is a succession of circles entwining each other.

Fret ornament is formed of straight lines like the wards of a key; used much by the Etruscans on their vases.

Mosaic ornament is a cemented inlay of marbles,

glass, shells, and rich varied stones; used in pavements, and on tops of tables.

Buhl ornament is an insertion of brass, and sometimes of wood, formed into foliages, flowers, animals, &c.

ORNAMENTS

USED IN CABINET AND UPHOLSTERY WORK,

When and where most applicable.

The ornamental, or decorative part of furniture, should be cautiously introduced; and when applied, should be designed with regularity and distinctness of outline; they should also be of a character simple, and appropriate to the work of which they are intended to form the embellishment.

You may lay it down as a general rule, that when a corresponding ornament cannot readily be adopted, one of an opposite character is not admissable; and in that case, an ornament of no peculiar character, is the only alternative.

In addition to the essential modifications of utility and convenience, the secondary objects, elegance and beauty, are indispensably necessary to be studied, to render each piece of furniture—what it should certainly be—a graceful, pleasing, and appropriate article.

Hall-chairs.—The family arms, or crest, carved tastefully, and emblazoned in their proper colours, form a most appropriate embellishment.

Library chairs.—Classic ornaments, such as the wreath of laurel, two genii striving for the bays, Minerva's bird, or others of a similar character, may be introduced with good effect.

Drawing-room chairs—Admit of an infinity of embellishment: Apollo's lyre, the Graces, tastefully devised scrolls, flowers, wreaths, and others of an appropriate description, may be executed either in buhl-work or in carved relief, as most suited to the character of the ornament chosen.

Card tables, being used for breakfast purposes, as well as for the evening party, may have the tea or coffee-plants for their ornaments, or the masks of Ceres, Bacchus, or Comus; but for a dining-table, the cornucopia, or some bold or chaste design of fruit, is decidedly the most appropriate. Stars and flowers have been introduced into this part of cabinet furniture; but a greater perversion of taste can be scarcely conceived.

Library and Writing tables should be embellished altogether from mythological history: the head of Mercury, placed on partitions between the drawers, are very appropriate, this god being said to be the inventor of letters: the caduceus is also well adapted for an ornament; so is the papyrus plant, from which paper was first made; the laurel-wreath, or the bays, may likewise be used; but no other tree, flower, or shrub should on any account be introduced, unless indeed we except the oak, the ink being made from the galls produced by this tree. Besides, Mercury, Apollo, the god of poetry, Cadmus, the inventor of part of the alphabet, and Clio, the presiding muse of history, are all appropriate embellishments, if applied with effect and in good taste.

Dining tables.—Broad ornaments are most consistent; the bread-tree and its fruit, form an admirable subject; hops, also, though a simple plant, form a very beautiful ornament when chased and inserted in wood. The masko of Ceres, with the corn in her hair, is also well suited to the dining-room.

Drawing-room tables may be properly embellished with any tastefully-designed ornament of fruits or flowers.

Sofas require, like the rest of the furniture, that their ornaments should be appropriate, chaste, and tasteful: the couch-flower, the heart's-ease, honeysuckles, eglantines, or Turkish ornaments, may be used with good effect; a greyhound couchant may adorn the end of the sofa.

Ottomans—Should be ornamented with the lyre, or with musical instruments or wreaths. Commodes are sometimes placed at each end of Ottomans; the pannels of which may be embellished with a winged figure of Victory, and the pedastals surmounted by two antique urns.

A dressing-table, or toilette, may be embellished with subjects chosen either from Mythology or Botany; the Graces, or foliage and flowers of scent-producing plants.

Window-seats in drawing-rooms.—The Egyptian lotus, or water-lily, or any flower characteristic of

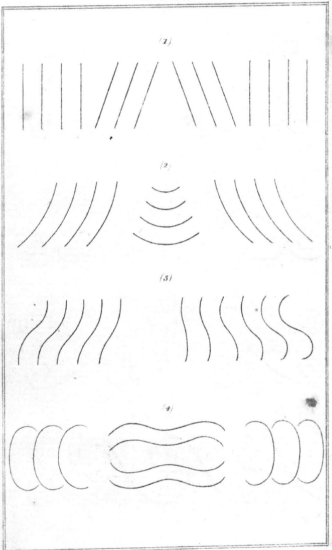

Simple & Compound Lines & Forms.

Compound Ornaments in Line & Shade.

Compound Ornaments in Line & Shade.

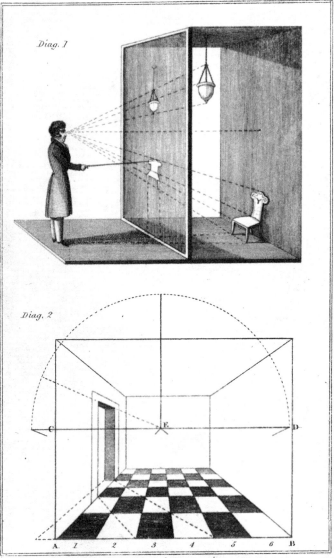

Diag. 1

Diag. 2

C   E   D

A.   1   2   3   4   5   6   B

Examples of Perspective.

Plate 7.

Fig. 2.

Fig. 1.

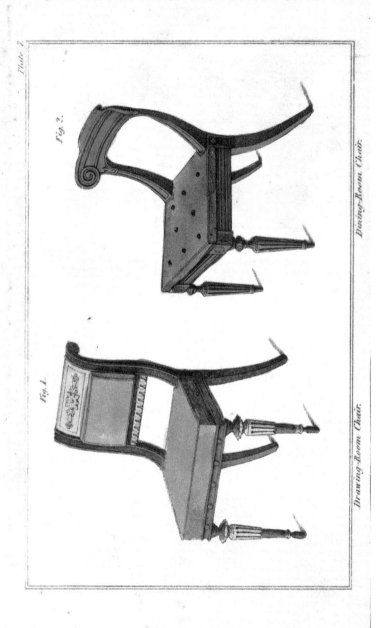

Dining-Room Chair.

Drawing-Room Chair.

Plate 9

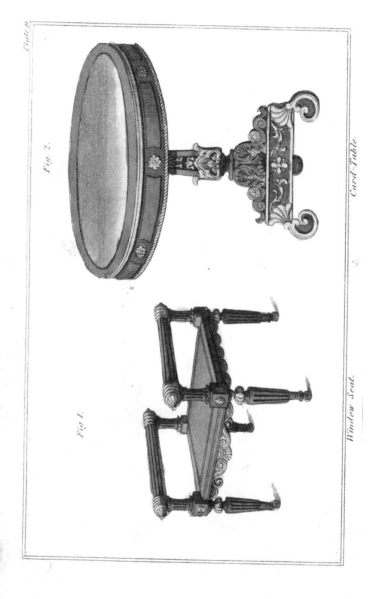

Fig. 2.

Fig. 1.

Card-Table.

Window Seat.

Plate III.

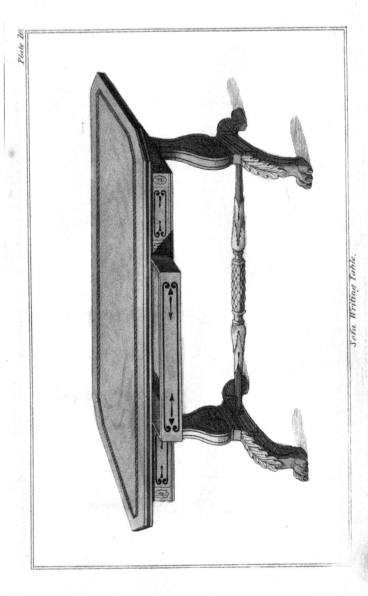

Sofa Writing Table.

Plate II

Circular Library Table.

Plate 12.

Sideboard and Wine Cooler.

Plate 13.

Grecian Couch & Footstool.

Plate 14.

Fig. 2.

Fig. 1.

Cheval Dressing-Glass.

Lady's Work-Table.

Plate 15.

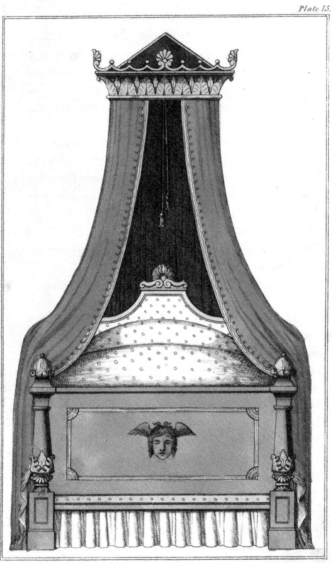

A French Bed.

rest and composure, may be very properly carved in wood, or inserted in buhl. English heart's-ease, and peony flowers, are of this cast. The mouldings, too, should be optically studied, that their whole contour may be visible below the eye, as well as when even with the horizon.

For cheval dressing glasses, the lotus, or water-lily, is admirably adapted; or the figure of Narcissus, viewing his own image in the water, would be very appropriate. For a pier commode and glass, chimeras: consoles, or turned pillars, are well suited. A laurel-wreath contended for by two genii, or the bust of Pallas, or Pluto, may be very consistently chosen for ladies' book-cases, with cabinet attached.

Sideboards may be adorned with the mask of Bacchus, or the horn of plenty; and on the backboard the thrysus, or sceptre of Bacchus, will form a very beautiful ornament; the celleret may have vine-leaves and clustered leaves, serpentined and festooned. Bacchanalian youths gathering grapes, if tastefully finished, would be an admirable ornament for this article of furniture.

The cot-bed admits a great variety of ornament. The head of Nox, the god of night; the stars, as her attendants: and a bunch of poppies, as producing sleep, may be all introduced with good effect; guardian genii or angels, doves, and many similar emblems, may be occasionally applied. White drapery, as emblamatical of infantile purity, is at all times most proper.

Bedsteads may be appropriately adorned with wreaths of nightshade, stars, a mask of Somnus, the starry hyacinth, the great Arabian star-flower, the poppy, or any other nocturnal plant or flower.

For drawing-room window-drapery, the embellishments to be chosen should be pine-apples, pomegranates, artichokes, or melons. The drapery, and testers, for drawing-rooms, should have flowers only, such as the passion-flower, the star of Bethlehem, or the rhododendron. The sun-flower looks well, but is rather common, and therefore unfit for to be introduced into elegant apartments.

Libraries should be finished in imitation of the antique, the embellishments should be of a strictly classical description. The owl and olive-branch, the laurel, Pegasus, the Olympic games, in relief, are very appropriate; or the twelve signs of the zodiac may be inlaid with mosaic work.

Fire-screens have a number of analogous ornaments; Jove's thunder-bolt, the Phœnix rising out of the flames, the cyclops, Vesta, the goddess of fire, or a representation of the fall of Phæton. These ornaments are equally appropriate for grates; as are also serpents vomiting forth fire. Fish or swans are applicable to a basin-stand; and an eagle to support a chandelier.

The preceding are some of the most tasteful and appropriate designs for the various articles of furniture described; and are intended to give the young cabinet-maker an insight into that most essential part of his business—the properly finishing and embellishing hi

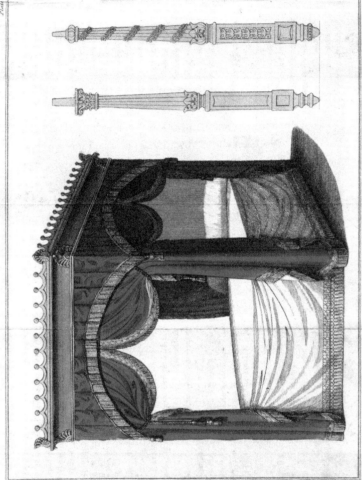

Plate 74

Four Post Bedstead, with Furniture and Drapery complete.

work with *appropriate* ornament only—a desideratum overlooked by too many workmen of the present day, some of whom it would appear seem more desirous to load their worth with ornament, than to study its fitness or appropriateness to the article in hand. A correct taste, a bold design, and a careful application, will ensure to a workman not only the respect of his employers, but will necessarily entail constant employ and liberal remuneration.

We shall close this part of our subject with several examples of articles of furniture and drapery, peculiarly applicable for subjects of study to the young student, as well as being useful to the more proficient Cabinet Maker and Upholsterer.

PART II.

VENEERING, INLAYING, &c.

OF VENEERING, INLAYING, AND EXECUTING IN BUHL-
WORK, THE ORNAMENTAL PART OF CABINET AND
UPHOLSTERY WORK.

VENEERING is the method of covering an inferior
wood with a surface of a very superior kind, so that
the parts of the article of furniture thus manufactured
which are presented to the eye, appear to the same
advantage as if the whole work were of the best description. If this be well performed, it is very durable,
looks well to the last, and is attainable at an expense
considerably less than a similar article would cost if
manufactured of the same wood throughout, but of
an inferior quality.

The principal requisite to ensure success in veneering,
is to select well-seasoned wood for the ground, and to
use the best and strongest glue. Be careful to exclude
the air in gluing on your veneer, or a blister will arise,
and spoil your work in that part. We need not add
any more to these remarks, as the following process
contains the most essential directions necessary in this
department.

Glueing and veneering as applicable to card and other table tops, secretary and book-case fronts, &c.

It is a desideratum among workmen to veneer their work in such a manner that it will stand. Several of the methods commonly used cause the piece either to warp in winding, or otherwise to get hollow, after the work is finished, on its upperside; and however careful the workman may be in laying his veneer, this will sometimes happen; much depends upon the manner of preparing the ground, perhaps more than in that of laying the veneer. Select that piece of deal which is freest from knots; slit it down the middle, or, take a piece out of the heart, and place the boards when cut to the required length in a warm place for two or three days; then joint them up, placing a heart edge and an outside edge together; when dry, cut your top again between each joint, and joint it afresh; you will then have a top glued up of pieces about two inches wide, and if you have been careful in making your joints good, you will have a top not so liable to cast after it is veneered, as many of the tops which are now done by the methods usually in practice.

You may use wainscot or other wood, instead of deal, but make your joints in the same manner. It is also a good plan, after having veneered your top, to lay it on the ground on some shavings, with the veneer downwards; it then dries gradually, and is much less likely to cast than by drying too quick.

To raise old veneers.

In repairing old cabinets and other furniture, work-men are sometimes at a loss to know how to get rid of those blisters which appear on the surface, in conse-quence of the glue under the veneer failing or causing the veneer to separate from the ground in patches; and these blisters are frequently so situated, that, without separating the whole veneer from the ground, it is impossible to introduce any glue between them to relay it; the great difficulty in this case is to separate the veneer from the ground without injuring it, as it ad-heres in many places too fast to separate without break-ing it. We will here, therefore, show how this operation may be performed without difficulty, and the veneer preserved perfectly whole and uninjured, ready for relaying as a new piece. First wash the surface with boiling water, and with a coarse cloth remove dirt or grease; then place it before the fire, or heat it with a caul; oil its surface with common linseed oil, place it again to the fire, and the heat will make the oil pene-trate quite through the veneer and soften the glue underneath; then whilst hot raise the edge gently with a chisel, and it will separate completely from the ground: be careful not to use too great force, or you will spoil your work; again, if it should get cold during the operation, apply more oil, and heat it again: re-peat this process till you have entirely separated the veneer; then wash off the old glue, and proceed to lay it again as a new veneer.

A strong glue, well suited for inlaying or veneering.

The best glue is readily known by its transparency, and being of a rather light brown, free from clouds and streaks. Dissolve this in water, and to every pint add half a gill of the best vinegar and half an ounce of isinglass.

To veneer tortoiseshell.

First, observe to have your shell of an equal thickness, and scrape and clean the under-side very smooth; grind some vermillion very fine, and mix it up with spirits of turpentine and varnish; lay two or three coats of colour on the under side of the shell, till it becomes opaque; when dry, lay it down with good glue.

BUHL WORK.

BUHL WORK is the art of inlaying in brass, silver, ivory, tortoiseshell, &c, and, if well executed, has an admirable effect. It was introduced into this country some years since, and is now brought to a state of perfection which equals any thing of foreign manufacture. It is now in very general use, and although almost a distinct branch of itself, it is certainly an essential part of cabinet work, and as such no workman should be entirely ignorant how to perform it.

Inlaying, as it is commonly termed, that is with fancy woods, has been too long in use to require any particular directions; buhl work is nothing more than inlaying in metals, turtle or tortoiseshell, ivory, or the like; and the chief difficulty seems to be in the method of cutting out the pieces for inlaying, and of introducing them in a proper manner as a veneer or inlay to the work. Our directions for sketching and drawing ornaments will here be of great use, and a careful attention to the following directions will enable the persevering and ingenious workmen to surmount every difficulty.

To prepare shell or brass ready for cutting out.

Being furnished with a thin piece of brass, of the thickness of a veneer, or as thin as can be conveniently worked, make the faces on both sides rough with a coarse file, or tooth plane; take also a veneer of shell of the dimensions requisite, tooth that also; then warm your plates and veneers, pass a coat of glue first over a plate of brass; place over that a thin sheet of paper; glue that, and place your shell veneer on the top; place them between two smooth and even boards, either kept down by a heavy weight, or squeezed tight together by hand-screws; let them remain till dry, and they will adhere together sufficiently for the following purpose.

Cutting out the pattern.

Draw the pattern on your shell: if not sufficiently plain, paste a piece of paper on its surface, and let it dry, on which draw your design; being now provided with a bow-saw, the blade of which is very thin and narrow, such as may be made with a watch spring, cut into about six strips, and the stretcher of the frame at a sufficient distance from the blade to enable you to turn in any direction, according to your pattern, and all made extremely light, begin by making a small hole in your veneer in a part where it will not so much be observed (unless the pattern comes quite out to the edge), and invert your saw; then very carefully follow the lines of your pattern till it is all cut through; you will then have two pieces, which may be separated by exposing them to steam or warm water; then take the two. corresponding pieces, one of brass and one of shell, and when glued together according to the following direction, you will have two veneers, the counterparts in pattern with other, only where the brass is in one, the shell will be in the other.

To glue up the patterns.

Take two boards of sufficient dimensions, and heat them before the fire; rub them well with tallow to prevent the glue sticking to it; then take a sheet of paper, on which lay your veneer, and having well rubbed some strong glue into the vacancies where the pattern is to be inserted, put it carefully in its place, rubbing it down with a veneering hammer, over which place another sheet of paper; place the whole between the hot boards, and press or screw them together with hand screws; let them get quite dry, they will come out quite clean from the boards, and appear as one piece of veneer; you may then scrape the paper clean

off, it is then ready for laying, or applying to your
work.

Laying your Veneer.

Having made your work perfectly level with a tooth-
plane, apply to your veneer the glue recommended in
page 43, and lay it on your work; then with a hot
board, termed a caul, fasten it well down by means of
hand-screws, and let it remain till perfectly hard. It
then only remains to be cleaned off and polished, according to the following directions.

In order to add to the beauty of your work, and
produce a variety in the shade, it is necessary, before
laying your veneer, to give that side intended to be
glued a coat or two of some colour ground in oil, or
varnish, and set by to dry thoroughly before you lay
your veneer, as red lead and vermillion ground together; king's yellow, Prussian blue, or any colour you
may fancy; and sometimes the surface is gilt on the side
which you intend to lay on your work; this produces a
very brilliant effect, and even the common Dutch metal
applied will have a very good effect.

The method here given for tortoise-shell and brass
is equally applicable to woods of two different colours,
only then you need not use any other glue but that in
common use, which must be good.

Inlaying with shaded wood.

Having shewn the methods of cutting out and veneering, we need now only shew the method used to

produce that shady brown edge, on works inlaid with white holly, and which, when well executed, has a very pleasing and ornamental effect; the method is as follows:

Into a shallow iron or tin-pot, put a sufficient quantity of fine dry sand, to be level with the top edge of it; place it on the fire till it is quite hot, then having your veneer cut out to the required pattern, dip the edges into the hot sand, and let them remain till the heat has made them quite brown; but be careful not to burn them; it is best to bring them to a proper colour, by repeatedly renewing the operation, than all at once, as you then do not injure the texture of the wood, and by immersing more or less of the edge, you produce a shaded appearance to your satisfaction. I would here recommend the workman, previous to beginning the operation, to have his pattern before him, shaded with umber, or any brown colour, in those parts that the wood is to be stained, as he then will be enabled, as he proceeds, to copy the various shades of the pattern, for the wood when once shaded cannot be altered; and as much of the beauty of this work depends on a proper judgment in placing your shadows, it is best always to have a guide to go by, that we may produce the best possible effect. Sometimes it is requisite to give a shadow in the centre, and not on the edge of your wood; and as this cannot be done by dipping it in the sand, you must do it by taking up a little of the hot sand, and sprinkling it, or heaping it up on those parts required to be darkened, letting it remain a short time, the shaking it off, and, if necessary, apply more where the colour is not deep enough.

To imitate inlaying of silver strings, &c.

This process is sometimes employed in the stocks, &c. of pistols, and if well executed has a very good effect; the first thing is to determine as to your pattern, which you must carefully draw upon your work, and then engrave, or cut away the different lines with sharp gouges, chisels, &c. so as to appear clean and even, taking care to cut them deep enough, and rather under, like a dovetail, to secure the composition afterwards to be put in the channels. The composition to resemble silver, may be made as follows: take any quantity of the purest and best grain tin, melt it in a ladle or other convenient receptacle: add to it, while in fusion, the purest quicksilver, stirring it to make it incorporate; when you have added enough, it will remain in a stiff paste; if too soft, add more tin, and if not sufficiently fluid, add quicksilver; grind this composition on a marble slab, or in a mortar, with a little size, and fill up the cuttings or grooves in your work, as you would with a piece of putty; let it remain some hours to dry, when you may polish it off with the palm of your hand, and it will appear as if your work was inlaid with silver. Instead of tin, you may make a paste of silver leaf and quicksilver, and proceed as above directed; you may also, for the sake of variety

in your work, rub in wax of different colours, and having levelled the surface and cleaned off your work, hold
it at a moderate distance from the fire, which will give
your strings a good gloss.

A glue for inlaying brass or silver strings, &c.

Melt your glue as usual, and to every pint add of
finely-powdered rosin and finely-powdered brick-dust
two spoonfuls each; incorporate the whole well together,
and it will hold the metal much faster than plain glue.

To polish brass ornaments inlaid in wood.

If your brass-work be very dull, file it with a small
smooth file; then polish it with a rubber of hat dipped
in Tripoli powder mixed with linseed oil, in the same
manner as you would polish varnish, until it has the
desired effect.

To wash brass figures over with silver.

Take one ounce of aqua-fortis, and dissolve in it over
a moderate fire one dram of good silver cut small, or
granulated; this silver being wholly dissolved, take the
vessel off the fire, and throw into it as much white
tartar as is required to absorb all the liquor. The residue
is a paste, with which you may rub over any work
made of copper, and which will give it the colour of
silver.

To imitate tortoise-shell on copper.

Rub copper laminas over with oil of nuts, then dry
them over a slow fire, supported by their extremities
upon small iron bars.

PART III.

DYING, STAINING, GILDING, &c.

OF DYING AND STAINING WOODS, IVORY, BONE, TOR-
TOISESHELL, MUSICAL INSTRUMENTS, AND ALL OTHER
MANUFACTURED ARTICLES; WITH THE PROCESS OF
SILVERING, GILDING, AND BRONZING.

* DYING wood is mostly applied for the purpose of
veneers, while staining is more generally had recourse
to, to give the desired colour to the article after
it has been manufactured.—In the one case the colour
should penetrate throughout; while in the latter, the
surface is all that is essential.

In dying, pear-tree, holly, and beech, take the best
black: but for most colours holly is preferable.—It is
also best to have your wood as young and as newly
cut as possible: After your veneers are cut, they should
be allowed to lie in a trough of water for four or five
days before you put them into the copper; as the water,
acting as a purgative to the wood, brings out abundance
of slimy matter; which, if not thus removed, the wood
will never be of a good colour; after this purificatory
process, they should be dried in the open air for at
least twelve hours; they are then ready for the copper.
By these simple means, the colour will strike much

quicker, and be of a brighter hue. It would also add
to the improvement of the colours, if, after your veneers
have boiled a few hours, they are taken out, dried in
the air, and again immersed in the colouring copper
Always dry veneers in the open air; for fire invariably
injures the colours.

Fine black.

Put six pounds of chip logwood into your copper,
with as many veneers as it will conveniently hold, without pressing too tight; fill it with water, and let it
boil *slowly* for about three hours; then add half a pound
of powdered verdigris, half a pound of copperas, and
four ounces of bruised nut-galls; fill the copper up with
vinegar as the water evaporates; let it boily gently two
hours each day, till the wood is dyed through.

Another method.

Procure some liquor from a tanner's pit, or make a
strong decoction of oak-bark, and to every gallon of
the liquor add a quarter of a pound of green copperas,
and mix them well together: put the liquor into the
copper, and make it quite hot, but not to boil; immerse
the veneers in it, and let them remain for an hour; take
them out, and expose them to the air till it has penetrated its substance; then add some logwood to the
solution, place your veneers again in it, and let
it simmer for two or three hours; let the whole
cool gradually, dry your veneers in the shade, and they
will have acquired a very fine black.

Fine blue.

Into a clean glass bottle, put one pound of oil of vitriol, and four ounces of the best indigo pounded in a mortar; (take care to set the bottle in a basin or earthen glazed pan, as it will ferment;) now put your veneers into a copper, or stone trough; fill it rather more than one-third with water, and add as much of the vitriol and indigo (stirring it about) as will make a fine blue, which you may know by trying it with a piece of white paper or wood; let the veneers remain till the dye has struck through.

The colour will be much improved, if the solution of indigo in vitriol be kept a few weeks before using it; you will also find the colour strike better if you boil your veneers in plain water till completely soaked through, and let them remain for a few hours to dry partially, previous to immersing them in the dye.

Another.

Throw pieces of quick lime into soft water; stir it well; when settled, strain or pour off the clear part, then to every gallon add ten or twelve ounces of the best turnsole; put the whole into your copper with your veneers, which should be of white holly, and prepared as usual by boiling in water; let them simmer gently till the colour has sufficiently penetrated, but be careful not to let them boil in it, as it would injure the colour.

A fine yellow.

Reduce four pounds of the root of barberry, by sawing, to dust, which put in a copper or brass trough; add four ounces of turmerick, and four gallons of water, then put in as many white holly veneers as the liquor will cover; boil them together for three hours, often turning them; when cool, add two ounces of aquafortis, and the dye will strike through much sooner.

A bright yellow.

To every gallon of water necessary to cover your veneers, add one pound of French berries; boil the veneers till the colour has penetrated through; add the following liquid to the infusion of the French berries, and let your veneers remain for two or three hours, and the colour will be very bright.

Liquid for brightening and setting colours.

To every pint of strong aqua-fortis, add one ounce of grain tin and a piece of sal-ammoniac, of the size of a walnut; set it by to dissolve, shake the bottle round with the cork out, from time to time: in the course of two or three days it will be fit for use. This will be found an admirable liquid to add to any colour, as it not only brightens it, but renders it less likely to fade from exposure to the air.

Bright green.

Proceed as in either of the above receipts to pro-

E 3

duce a yellow; but instead of adding aqu'-fortis, or the
brightening liquid, add as much vitriolated indigo (page
52) as will produce the desired colour.

Another green.

Dissolve four ounces of the best verdigris, and sap green
and indigo half an ounce each, in three pints of the
best vinegar; put in your veneers, and gently boil till
the colour has penetrated sufficiently.

The hue of the green may be varied by altering the
proportion of the ingredients; and I should advise, unless
wanted for a particular purpose, to leave out the sap
green, as it is a vegetable colour very apt to change, or
turn brown, when exposed to the air.

Bright red.

To two pounds of genuine Brazil dust, add four
gallons of water; put in as many veneers as the liquid
will cover; boil them for three hours; then add two
ounces of alum, and two ounces of aqua-fortis, and keep
it lukewarm until it has struck through.

Another red.

To every pound of logwood chips add two gallons of
water; put in your veneers, and boil as in the last;
then add a sufficient quantity of the brightening liquid
(page 53) till you see the colour to your mind; keep the
whole as warm as you can bear your finger in it, till the
colour has sufficiently penetrated.

The logwood chips should be picked from all foreign substances, with which it generally abounds, as bark, dirt, &c. and it is always best when fresh cut, which may be known by its appearing of a bright red colour; for if stale it will look brown, and not yield so much colouring matter.

Purple.

To two pounds of chip logwood and half a pound of Brazil dust, add four gallons of water, and after putting in your veneers; boil them for at least three hours; then add six ounces of pearl-ash and two ounces of alum; let them boil two or three hours every day, till the colour has struck through.

The Brazil dust only contributes to make the purple of a more red cast; you may therefore omit it, if you require a deep blush purple.

Another purple.

Boil two pounds of logwood, either in chips or powder, in four gallons of water with your veneers; after boiling till the colour is well struck in, add by degrees vitriolated indigo (see page 52) till the purple is of the shade required, which may be known by trying it with a piece of paper; let it then boil for one hour, and keep the liquid in a milk-warm state till the colour has penetrated the veneer. This method, when properly managed, will produce a brilliant purple, not so likely to fade as the foregoing.

Orange.

Let the veneers be dyed, by either of the methods given in page 53, of a fine deep yellow, and while they are still wet and saturated with the dye, transfer them to the bright red dye as in page 54, till the colour penetrates equally throughout.

Silver grey.

Expose to the weather in a cast-iron pot of six or eight gallons, old iron nails, hoops, &c. till covered with rust; add one gallon of vinegar, and two of water, boil all well for an hour; have your veneers ready, which must be air-wood (not too dry,) put them in the copper you use to dye black, and pour the iron liquor over them; add one pound of chip logwood, and two ounces of bruised nut-galls; then boil up another pot of the iron liquor to supply the copper with, keeping the veneers covered, and boiling two hours a day, till of the required colour.

Another grey.

Expose any quantity of old iron, or what is better, the borings of gun barrels, &c. in any convenient vessel, and from time to time, sprinkle them with spirits of salt (muriatic acid,) diluted in four times its quantity of water, till they are very thickly covered with rust; then to every six pounds add a gallon of water, in which has been dissolved two ounces of salt of tartar; lay your veneers in the copper, and cover them with this liquid; let it boil for two or three hours till well soaked, then to every gallon of liquor add a quarter of a pound of green copperas, and keep the whole at a moderate temperature till the dye has sufficiently penetrated.

STAINING.

STAINING wood is altogether a different process from dying it, and requires no preparation before the stain be applied : it is peculiarly useful to bedstead and chair makers. In preparing the stain, but little trouble is required; and, generally speaking, its application differs very little from that of painting. When carefully done, and properly varnished, staining has a very beautiful appearance, and is much less likely to meet with injury than japanning.

Black stain for immediate use.

Boil half a pound of chip logwood in two quarts of water, add one ounce of pearl-ash, and apply it hot to the work with a brush. Then take half a pound of logwood, boil it as before in two quarts of water, and add half an ounce of verdigris and half an ounce of copperas; strain it off, put in half a pound of rusty steel filings, with this go over your work a second time.

To stain beech a mahogany colour.

Put two ounces of dragon's blood, broken in pieces, into a quart of rectified spirits of wine; let the bottle stand in a warm place, shake it frequently; when dissolved, it is fit for use.

Another method for a black stain.

Boil one pound of logwood in four quarts of water, add a double handful of walnut-peel or shells, boil it up again, take out the chips, add a pint of the best vinegar, and it will be fit for use; apply it boiling hot.

This will be improved, if, when dry, you apply a solution of green copperas dissolved in water, (an ounce to a quart), hot over your first stain.

To imitate rose-wood.

Boil half a pound of logwood, in three pints of water till it is of a very dark red, add half an ounce of salt of tartar. While boiling hot, stain your wood with two or three coats, taking care that it is nearly dry between each; then with a stiff flat brush, such as is used by the painters for graining, form streaks with the black stain above-named, which, if carefully executed, will be very nearly the appearance of dark rosewood.

Another method.

Stain with the black stain; and when dry, with a brush as above, dipped in the brightening liquid (see page 53), form red veins in imitation of the grain of rosewood, which will produce a beautiful effect.

A handy brush for the purpose, may be made out of a flat brush, such as is used for varnishing; cut the sharp points off, and make the edges irregular, by cutting out a few hairs here and there, and you will have a tool which, will accurately imitate the grain.

To imitate king or botany-bay wood.

Boil half a pound of French berries in two quarts of water, till of a deep yellow, and, while boiling hot, give two or three coats to your work; when nearly dry, form the grain with the black stain, which must also be used hot.

You may, for variety, to heighten the colour, after giving it two or three coats of yellow, give one of strong logwood liquor, and then use the black stain as directed.

Red stain for bedsteads and common chairs.

Archil, as sold at the shops, will produce a very good stain of itself, when used cold; but if, after one or two coats being applied and suffered to get almost dry, it is brushed over with a hot solution of pearl-ash in water, it will improve the colour.

To improve the colour of any stain.

Mix in a bottle one ounce of nitric acid, half a teaspoonful of muriatic acid, a quarter of an ounce of grain tin, and two ounces of rain-water. Mix it at least two days before using, and keep your bottle well corked.

To stain horn in imitation of tortoise-shell.

Mix an equal quantity of quick-lime and red-lead with strong soap lees, lay it on the horn with a small brush, in imitation of the mottle of tortoise-shell; when dry, repeat it two or three times.

To stain ivory or bone red.

Boil shavings of scarlet cloth in water, and add by degrees pearl-ashes till the colour is extracted, a little roach alum, now added, will clear the colour; then strain it through a linen cloth. Steep your ivory or bone in aqua-fortis (nitrous acid) diluted with twice its quantity of water; then take it out, and put it into your scarlet dye till the colour is to your mind; be careful not to let your aqua-fortis be too strong, neither let your ivory remain too long in it; try it first with a slip of ivory, and if you observe the acid has just caused a trifling roughness on its surface, take it out immediately, and put it into the red liquid, which must be warm, but not too hot; a little practice, with these cautions, will enable you to succeed according to your wishes; cover the places you wish to remain unstained with white wax, and the stain will not penetrate in those places, but leave the ivory of its natural colour.

To stain ivory or bone black.

Add to any quantity of nitrate of silver (lunar caustic), three times its bulk of water, and steep your ivory or bone in it; take it out again in about an hour, and expose it to the sun-shine to dry, and it will be a perfect black.

To stain ivory or bone green.

Steep your work in a solution of verdigris and sal-ammoniac in weak aqua-fortis, in the proportion of two parts of the former to one of the latter, being careful to use the precautions mentioned for staining red, in page 66.

To stain ivory, &c. blue.

Stain your materials green according to the previous process, and then dip them in a strong solution of pearl-ash and water.

To stain ivory, &c. yellow.

Put your ivory in a strong solution of alum in water, and keep the whole some time nearly boiling; then take them out and immerse them in a hot mixture of turmeric and water, either with or without the addition of French berries; let them simmer for about half an hour, and your ivory will be of a beautiful yellow.—Ivory or bone should dry very gradually, or it will split or crack.

TO STAIN MUSICAL INSTRUMENTS.
Fine crimson.

BOIL one pound of good Brazil dust in three quarts of water for an hour; strain it, and add half an ounce of cochineal; boil it again gently for half an hour, and it will be fit for use.

If you would have it more of a scarlet tint, boil half an ounce of saffron in a quart of water, for an hour, and pass over the work previous to the red stain.

Purple.

To a pound of good chip logwood, put three quarts

F

of water, boil it well for an hour; then add four ounces
of pearl-ash, and two ounces of indigo pounded.

Fine black.

In general, when black is required in musical instruments, it is produced by japanning; the work being
well prepared with size and lamp black, apply the
black japan (as sold at the varnish-makers), after
which, varnish and polish.

But as a black stain is sometimes required for finger-
boards, bridges, and flutes, you may then proceed as directed in staining, but the wood ought to be either pear,
apple, or box-wood; the latter is preferable; and if it
be rubbed over, when dry, with a rag or flannel dipped
in hot oil, it will give it a gloss equal to ebony.

Fine blue.

Into a pound of oil of vitriol (sulphuric acid) in a
clean glass phial, put four ounces of indigo, and proceed as above-directed in dying purple.

Fine green.

To three pints of the strongest vinegar, add four
ounces of the best verdigris pounded fine, half an ounce
of sap green, and half an ounce of indigo.

Distilled vinegar, or verjuice, improves the colour.

Bright yellow.

You need not stain wood yellow, as a small piece of
aloes put into the varnish, will have all the desired
effect.

To stain box wood brown.

Hold your work to the fire that it may receive a gentle warmth; then take aqua-fortis, and with a feather pass over the work till you find it change to a fine brown (always keeping it near the fire) ; you may then oil and polish it.

SILVERING AND GILDING.

THE art of silvering, as applied to cabinet work, is precisely similar to that of gilding ; the directions for the one will therefore be the instructions for the other, with little other variation than using silver-leaf instead of gold-leaf;—silvering for plate glass, is a trade by itself, and is too troublesome and expensive a process, except where carried on in extensive way, to be introduced in a work, where its place can be occupied with matter more useful to the cabinet-maker.

There are two methods of gilding ;—that for out-door work, to stand the weather, or to wash, is called oil gilding; this is performed by means of oil or varnish. The other, called burnish-gilding, is the most beautiful, and best adapted for fine work, as frames, articles of furniture, &c. or as applied by the cabinet-maker, in the internal decoration of rooms, or the carved work of its furniture. Both these methods are so essential to the ingenious workman, that we shall give him every instruction necessary to perform his work in the best manner.

The requisites necessary to be provided with.

First, a sufficient quantity of leaf-gold, which is of two sorts, the deep gold, as it is called, and the pale gold; the former is the best; the latter very useful, and may occasionally be introduced for variety or effect.

Secondly, A gilder's cushion; an oblong piece of wood, covered with rough calf-skin, stuffed with flannel several times doubled, with a border of parchment, about four inches deep at one end, to prevent the air blowing the leaves about when placed on the cushion.

Thirdly, A gilding knife, with a straight and very smooth edge, to cut the gold.

Fourthly, Several camel-hair pencils in sizes, and tips, made of a few long camel's hairs put between two cards in the same manner as hairs are put into tin cases for brushes, thus making a flat brush with a very few hairs.

Lastly, A burnisher, which is a crooked piece of agate set in a long wooden handle.

Size for oil gilding.

Grind calcined red ochre with the best and oldest drying oil, and mix with it a little oil of turpentine when used.

When you intend to gild your work, first give it a coat of parchment-size; then apply the above size where requisite, either in patterns or letters, and let it remain till by touching it with your fingers it feels just sticky; then apply your gold-leaf, and dab it on with a piece of cotton; in about an hour wash off the superfluous gold with a sponge and water; and, when dry, varnish it with copal varnish.

To make size for preparing frames, &c.

To half a pound of parchment shavings, or cuttings of white leather, add three quarts of water, and boil it in a proper vessel till reduced to nearly half the quantity; then take it off the fire, and strain it through a sieve: be careful in the boiling to keep it well stirred, and do not let it burn.

To prepare frames or wood-work.

First, with the above alone, and boiling-hot, go over your frames in every part; then mix a sufficient quantity of whiting with size, to the consistency of thick cream, with which go over every part of your frame, six or seven times, carefully letting each coat dry before you proceed with the next, and you will have a white ground fit for gilding on, nearly or quite the sixteenth of an inch in thickness.

Your size must not be too thick, and when mixed with the whiting should not be put on so hot as the first coat is by itself: it will be better to separate the dirty or coarse parts of the whiting, by straining it through a sieve.—Vauxhall whiting is the best.

Polishing.

When the prepared frames are quite dry, clean and polish them; to do this, wet a small piece at a time, and with a smooth fine piece of cloth dipped in water,

rub the part till all the bumps and inequalities are removed, and for those parts where the fingers will not
enter, as the mouldings, &c. wind the wet cloth round
a piece of wood, and by this means make the surface
all smooth and even alike.

Where there is carved work, &c. it will sometimes
be necessary to bring the mouldings to their original
sharpness, by means of chisels, gouges, &c. as the preparation will be apt to fill up all the finer parts of the
work, which must be thus restored; it is sometimes
the practice, after polishing, to go over the work once
with fine yellow or Roman ochre, but this is rarely
necessary.

Gold-size.

Grind fine bol-ammoniac well with a muller and
stone: scrape into it a little beef suet, and grind all
well together; after which, mix in with a pallet knife a
small proportion of parchment size with a double proportion of water.

Another gold-size.

Grind a lump of tobacco-pipe clay into a very stiff
paste with thin size; add a small quantity of ruddle,
and fine black lead ground very fine, and temper the
whole with a small piece of tallow.

To prepare your frames, &c. for gilding.

Take a small cup, or pipkin, into which put as much
gold-size as you judge sufficient for the work in hand,
add parchment-size, till it will just flow from the brush;

when quite hot, pass over your work with a very soft brush, taking care not to put the first coat too thick; let it dry, and repeat it twice or three times more, and when quite dry, brush the whole with a stiff brush, to remove any remaining nobs. Your work is now ready for applying the gold.

Your parchment-size should be of such a consistence, when cold, as the common jelly sold in the shops; for if too thick it will be apt to chip, and if too thin it will not have sufficient body.

Laying on the gold.

This is the most difficult part of the operation, and requires some practice; but with a little caution and attention, it may be easily performed.

Turn your gold out of the book on your cushion a leaf at a time; then passing your gilding knife under it, bring it into a convenient part of your cushion for cutting it into the size of the pieces required; breathe gently on the centre of the leaf, and it will lay flat on your cushion; then cut it to your mind by bringing the knife perpendicularly over it, and sawing it gently till divided.

Place your work before you in a position nearly horizontal, and with a long-haired camel-hair pencil, dipped in water (or with a small quantity of brandy in the water), go over as much of your work as you intend the piece of gold to cover; then take up your gold from your cushion with your tip; by drawing it over your forehead, or cheek, it will damp it sufficiently to

adhere to the gold, which must then be carefully trans-
ferred to your work, and gently breathing on it, it will
adhere; but take care that the part you apply it to is
sufficiently wet; indeed, it must be floating, or you will
find the gold apt to crack: proceed in this manner by a
little at a time, and do not attempt to cover too much
at once, till by experience you are able to handle the
gold with freedom. Be careful, in proceeding with your
work, if you find any flaws, or cracks appear, to take a
corresponding piece of gold, and apply it immediately;
sometimes, also, you will find it necessary, when your
gold does not appear to adhere sufficiently tight, to
draw a pencil quite filled with water close to the edge of
the gold, that the water may run underneath it, which
will answer your expectation.

Burnishing.

When your work is covered with gold, set it by to
dry, it will be ready to burnish in about eight or ten
hours; but it will depend on the warmth of the room
or state of the air, and practice will enable you to judge
of the proper time.

When it is ready, those parts which you intend to
burnish must be dusted with a soft brush, and wiping
your burnisher with a piece of soft wash-leather (quite
dry), begin to burnish about an inch or two in length at
a time, taking care not to lean too hard, but with a
gentle and quick motion apply the tool till you find it
equally bright all over.

Matting, or dead gold.

Those parts of your work which look dull from not being burnished, are now to be matted, that is, are to be made to look like dead gold; for if left in its natural state it will have a shining appearance, which must be thus rectified:

Grind some vermillion, or yellow ochre, very fine, and mix a very small portion either with the parchment-size or with the white of an egg, and with a very soft brush lay it even and smooth on the parts intended to look dull; if well done, it will add greatly to the beauty of the work.

The work must be well cleared of superfluous gold, by means of a soft brush, previous to burnishing or matting.

Finishing.

It is now only necessary to touch the parts in the hollows with a composition made by grinding vermillion, gamboge, and red lead, very fine, with oil of turpentine, and applying it carefully with a small brush in the parts required, and your work is completed.

Sometimes the finishing is done by means of shell-gold, which is the best method; it should be diluted with gum-arabic, and applied with a small brush.

To make shell gold.

Take any quantity of leaf gold, and grind it, with a small portion of honey, to a fine powder; add a little gum-arabic and sugar-candy, with a little water, and mix it well together: put it in a shell to dry against you want it.

Silver Size.

Take tobacco-pipe clay, grind it fine with a little black lead and Genoa soap, and add parchment-size as directed for the gold-size.

Note.—Any soap would most probably answer as well as Genoa soap; but it is here directed, as it has been found to answer very well.

Silvering.

Silvering is at present but little in use, though some old works still look very well, and it might be introduced with advantage in many works; the great fault is, that it is apt to tarnish; but may be preserved, with very little diminution to its beauty, by applying a thin coat of the cleanest copal or mastic varnish. The process for silvering is exactly the same as for gilding; but the matting must be done by mixing a small quantity of flake white in powder, with a little Prussian blue (just sufficient to tinge it) along with plain size or white of egg.

To make liquid foil for silvering glass globes, bent mirrors, &c.

To half an ounce of lead, add half an ounce of fine tin, and melt them together in an iron ladle: when in a state of fusion, add half an ounce of bismuth; skim off the dross, remove the ladle from the fire, and before it cools, add five ounces of quicksilver, and stir the whole well together, observing not to breathe over it, as the evaporation of the silver is very pernicious.

In mixing, avoid breathing the fumes that evaporate, as it is a poison of the most deadly nature.

Another method.

To four ounces of quicksilver, put as much tin foil as will become barely fluid when mixed; have your globe clean and warm, and inject the quicksilver by means of a clean earthen pipe at the aperture, turning it about till it is silvered all over; let the remainder run out, and hang it up.

An excellent receipt to burnish gold size.

One ounce of black lead, ground very fine, one ounce of deer suet, one ounce of red chalk, and one pound or pipe-clay, ground with weak parchment-size to a stiff consistency, to be used as directed in the article ' Size for oil gilding,' page 64.

To gild leather for bordering doors, folding screens, &c.

Damp a clear brown sheep-skin with a sponge and water, and strain it tight, with tacks, on a board sufficiently large; when dry, size it with clear double size; then beat the whites of eggs, with a whisk, to a foam, and let them stand to settle; then take books of leaf silver, a sufficient quantity, and blow out the leaves of silver on a gilder's cushion; pass over the leather carefully with the egg size, and with a tip brush lay on the silver, closing any blister with a bit of cotton; when dry, varnish them over with yellow lacker till they are of a fine gold colour. Your skin being thus gilt, you may then cut it into strips as you please, and join with paste to any length.

Perform the foregoing operation in the height of summer, when the air is clear, dry, and warm, that the skin may dry well before you size it, and the size may have the desired effect upon the pores, and no farther, and the silver will not tarnish before you lacker it.

To gild the borders of leather tops of library tables, work boxes, &c.

The tops of library tables, &c. are usually covered with Morocco leather, and ornamented with a gilt border, and are usually sent to the book-binder for that purpose. The method by which they perform it is as follows:—They first go over that part intended to be gilt with a sponge dipped in the glare of eggs, which is the whites beaten up to a froth and left to settle; and the longer made or older it is, so much the better; then being provided with a brass-roller, on the edge of which the pattern is engraved, and fixed as a wheel in a handle, they place it before the fire till heated so that, by applying a wetted finger, it will just hiss; while it is heating, rub the part with an oiled rag, or clean tallow, where the pattern is intended to be, and lay strips of gold on it, pressing it down with cotton;

then with a steady hand run the roller along the edge
of the leather, and wipe the superfluous gold off with an
oiled rag, and the gold will adhere in those parts where
the impression of the roller has been, and the rest will
rub off with the oiled rag.

BRONZING.

THE art of Bronzing is equally useful to the cabinet-
maker as the smith, the carved and turned work in furniture being frequently finished in imitation of bronze;
and if well done, has a very elegant effect, and adds
much to the beauty of the article. It is by no means a
difficult process; but nevertheless requires considerable
care and judgment to arrive at perfection.

To bronze figures.

For the ground, after it has been sized and rubbed
down, in a similar manner as if for gilding, take
Prussian blue, verditer, and spruce ochre, grind them
separately in water, turpentine, or oil, according to the
work; mix them together in such proportions as will
produce the colour you desire; then grind Dutch
metal, commonly called bronze, in the same material
you ground your colour; laying it on the prominent
parts of the figure, and, if done with care, it will produce a grand effect.

There are several different colours of bronze, which
are best imitated by the powders sold at almost all
colour-shops, called bronze-powders, independent of

the one here mentioned of Dutch metal, which it will be best to purchase, as they are made, not without considerable trouble, by dissolving different metals in aqua-fortis, and precipitating the solution by means of sal-ammoniac, and washing the precipitate in water, and drying it on blotting-paper. The ingenious artist will suit the colour of the bronze, by mixing corre-sponding colours of paint for a ground.

To bronze on wood.

Having stained those parts intended for bronzing black, by any of the methods shewn under the article *staining*, take japanners' gold size, and mix with a small portion of Roman ochre and Prussian blue, go over the blacked parts lightly, then suffer it to dry till it feels just stickey to the finger, but not to come off, then with a hard ball of cotton, dipped in any of the bronze powders, rub those places that are prominent, and, if you think proper, give it a thin coat of japan-ners' gold size thinned with spirits of turpentine; or you may alter the colour of your bronze by mixing either more or less blue, as also other colours, as ver-diter green by itself, but do not put your colour on thick over the black stain, but rather glaze it on, for it is not wanted in a body, but should be rather tran-sparent, as it makes it more of a metallic appearance.

To bronze brass figures for ornaments.

After having lackered your brass work in those parts you wish to look like gold, take for those parts that are intended to appear as bronze, any quantity of umbers either burnt or in its natural state, according to the colour you require, and grind it with a small quantity of spirits of wine: do the same with verditer, and also spruce ochre, keep these colours separate for use, and when wanted take some pale gold lacker, and mix with it a portion of these ingredients till you get the colour required; then apply this mixture in the same manner as directed in lackering brass work, (page 76); you may also mix with it any coloured bronze powder for the sake of variety.—A little experience, and a few experiments with these compositions, will enable the workman to imitate any bronze colour he pleases.

PART IV.

LACKERING, JAPANNING, VARNISHING,
&c. &c.

OF LACKERING, JAPANNING, VARNISHING, AND POLISH-
ING CABINET AND UPHOLSTERY WORK GENERALLY.

LACKERING.

AMONG the arts that lend their assistance to the cabinet-maker in the completion of many of his articles
of furniture, that of lackering must not be forgotten:
to do what the cabinet-maker may require, few directions are necessary, it being a simple and easy process.

To lacker brass work.

If the work is old, clean it first, according to the
directions hereafter given; but if new, it will merely
require being freed from dust, and rubbed with a piece
of wash leather to make it as bright as possible. Put
your work on a hot iron plate, (or the hob of your fire-
place will be a good substitute) till it is moderately
heated, but not too hot, or it will blister your lacker;
then, according to the colour you wish, take of the
following preparations, and making it warm, lay hold
of your work with a pair of pincers or pliers, and with
a soft brush apply the lacker, being careful not to rub

it on, but stroke the brush gently one way, and place your work on the hot plate again, till the varnish is hard; but do not let it remain too long: experience will best tell you when it should be removed; some, indeed, do not place it on the stove or plate a second time; if it should not be quite covered, you may repeat it carefully, and if pains be taken with your lacker, will look equal to metal gilt.

To make gold lacker for brass.

Rectified spirits of wine, half a pint; mix half a pound of seed-lac picked clean, and clear of all pieces, (as upon that depends the beauty of the lacker) with the spirits of wine; keep them in a warm place, and shake them repeatedly; when the seed-lac is quite dissolved, it is fit for use.

Another lacker.

Take of the clearest and best seed-lac, a quarter of a pound, and of dragon's-blood a quarter of an ounce; pound them well together; add a gill and a half of the best spirits of wine; set it in a warm place to dissolve; strain it, and it is fit for use.

Superior lacker for brass.

Take of seed-lac three ounces; amber or copal, ground on porphyry, one ounce; dragon's-blood twenty grains, extract of red sandal wood fifteen grains, oriental saffron eighteen grains, very pure alcohol twenty ounces.

To apply this varnish to ornaments or articles of brass, expose them to a gentle heat, and dip them into the varnish; two or three coatings may be applied in this manner, if necessary. The varnish is durable, and has a beautiful colour. Articles varnished in this manner may be cleansed with water and a bit of dry rag.

Pale gold lacker.

Dissolve in a quarter of a pint of spirits of wine as much gamboge as will give it a bright yellow, then add three ounces of seed-lac, finely powdered and sifted, set it in a sand-bath to dissolve; when that is the case, bottle and stop it well till wanted for use.

Lacker with spirits of turpentine.

Take seed-lac two ounces, sandarac, or mastic, two ounces, dragon's-blood a quarter of an ounce, gum gutte twenty grains, clear turpentine one ounce, and the best spirits of turpentine sixteen ounces.

This lacker, though certainly not equal to those made with spirits of wine, is, from its cheapness, often very useful for the more common purposes; it does not dry so quick, nor is it so durable; but for such purposes as lackering silvered leather, &c. it answers very well. We may here remark, that we may vary the colour of our lackers, by using more or less, or altering the pro-portion of the colouring material; and at the same time, notice that all the colouring substances that are of a resinous quality, or that will give out their colouring matter when infused in spirits, are proper to be used in the composition of lacker; we may, therefore, make lackers of almost any colour, by selecting different colouring materials, and mixing them with the other compositions used as the basis of all lackers, such as seed-lac, shell-lac, &c.

To clean old brass-work for lackering.

Make a strong lye of wood ashes, which may be strengthened by soap-lees; put in your brass-work, and the lacker will soon come off; then have ready a mixture of aqua-fortis and water, sufficiently strong to take off the dirt; wash it afterwards in clean water, and lacker it with such of the above compositions as may be most suitable to your work.

JAPANNING.

JAPANNING is generally performed by persons brought up to the practice of the art exclusively; but as it frequently happens that japanned work receives damage, when it is very inconvenient (either from distance or other circumstances) to send for a japanner to repair it, it may not be improper to lay down the most simple methods used in that branch.

Take care to provide yourself with a small muller and stone, to grind any colour you may require; and observe that all your wood-work must be prepared with size, and some coarse material mixed with it to fill up and harden the grain of the wood (such as may best

suit the colour intended to be laid on), which must be
rubbed smooth with glass paper when dry; but in cases
of accident, it is seldom necessary to re-size the damaged places, unless they are considerable.

Always grind your colours smooth in spirits of turpentine; then add a small quantity of turpentine and
spirit-varnish; lay it carefully on with a camel-hair
brush, and varnish it with brown or white spirit-var
nish, according to the colour.

You will also find a box filled with currier's shavings
useful for cleaning your stones and pallet with, for they
should never be laid by dirty, as the beauty of the work
depends a great deal on keeping all your colours separated: therefore before you grind another colour, the
first should be well wiped off your stone.

For a black japan.

Mix a little gold size and lamp-black: it will bear a
good gloss without varnishing over.

To imitate black rosewood.

The work must be grounded black, after which well
grind some red lead, mixed up as before directed, which
lay on with a flat stiff brush, in imitation of the streaks
in the wood; after which take a small quantity of lake,
ground fine, and mix it with brown spirit-varnish, carefully observing not to have more colour in it than will
just tinge the varnish: but should it on trial be still
too red, assist it with a little umber ground very fine;

with which pass over the whole of the work intended
to imitate black rose-wood, and it will have the desired
effect.

If well done, when it is varnished and polished, it
will scarcely be known from rose-wood.

Instead of the umber in the above, you may use a
small quantity of Vandyke brown; it is much more
transparent than the umber.

INDIA JAPANNING.

THE great peculiarity in the Indian method is the
embossing, or raising the figures, &c. above the surface
or ground, and the metallic, or bronze-like hue of the
several designs; the grotesque appearance of the several ornaments, whether figures, landscapes, or whatever
other designs they are embellished with, being so totally
different from every principle of perspective, and so
opposite to every idea we have of correct drawing.
Nothing but the study of Chinese models themselves
will enable the workman to imitate with any degree of
precision their several characteristics. We can, therefore, only give such directions for preparing the ground,
embossing the designs, and producing the peculiar effect of Chinese japan, as will enable the ingenious
mechanic to execute any work of the kind, with truth
and accuracy, according to any copy given, while it
must remain with him to use his taste and judgment in
effecting a likeness which will characterize this peculiar manufacture.

Ground for Chinese japan.

Mix any quantity of the finest whiting to the consistency of paint with isinglass size; lay on your wood two or three coats, observing to put it on evenly and smoothly, and not too thick; let it dry; then rub it gently with a soft rag and water till the surface is quite level and polished: if you add a small portion of honey to the mixture, it will render it less liable to crack or peel off.   If your ground is to be black, which is the most usual one, give it a coat or two of the black japan mentioned in the common method of japanning, and it is prepared for your figures, &c.

Another ground.

Mix fine plaster of Paris with size not too thick, and apply it quickly, for it soon gets hard: two coats in most instances will be sufficient; after it is quite dry, polish it with fine glass paper, and rub it with a wet soft cloth; then give it two or three coats of drying linseed oil, or as much as it will soak up; when dry it is ready for japanning.

To make black japan.

Grind ivory or lamp-black very fine with turpentine, add a little lac varnish or copal varnish, and temper it to a proper consistency with varnish for laying on your ground; give your work two or three coats at least, using a gentle heat, as directed in varnishing.

To trace your design on the ground.

Having drawn the figures on a piece of white paper either with ink or pencil, rub the back of it with fine chalk or whiting, and shake all the loose powder off; lay it on your ground, and trace or go over every part of your outline with the end of a blunt bodkin, or other similar instrument; you will then have a sketch in faint outline on your ground; you may then proceed to put in your figures, &c. with any colour you wish, or bronze them.

To raise figures on your work.

Prepare a mixture of whiting and size, (some prefer the whites of eggs,) of a consistency to flow freely from your pencil, the hairs of which must be rather long. Begin with a figure, or other part, but do not do too much at a time, and trace the outline correctly with a free hand; then take a piece of stick pointed at the end, dip it into your composition, and fill up the inside of your outline; continue to put more of the mixture on till it is raised sufficiently above the surface; let it get quite dry, and then polish it with a soft camel-hair pencil and clean water, which will make it perfectly smooth and level. Care must be taken in this process, that your composition is not too thin, or it will spread beyond the bounds of your outline, but just so thick as to drop from the stick; some mix with the whiting a portion of flake white, or dry white lead. This is an improvement, and for very particular work should be adopted.

BRONZES PECULIARLY ADAPTED FOR INDIA JAPANNING,
AND SIMILAR PURPOSES.

Gold bronze.

Put any quantity of gold-leaf into a stone mortar, together with a small portion of honey, and a little water; grind them well together, till the gold seems dispersed throughout the whole paste; add by degrees more water till it is quite thin, keeping it continually stirred; let it settle, and pour the water off as near as you can without wasting your gold; repeat the washing till you see the gold in the form of a fine powder at the bottom; then pour the water clean off, and turn the gold out on a piece of blotting paper, keep it from the dust, and when all the moisture is evaporated put it into a bottle for use.

This is a very expensive bronze, and used only for those works which are very particular; but a very good substitute may be had by treating Dutch metal in the same manner, but be sure to keep this close stopped, or it is very apt to tarnish.

Copper bronze.

Put some very fine filings of copper into an iron mortar, and beat them the same as that of the gold leaf or Dutch metal; instead of using honey, you may pound it dry with a portion of sal-ammoniac, and then wash it as above; keep this also from the air. Brass filings may be treated in the same manner.

Silver bronze

May be made with silver leaf treated in the same manner as directed for gold: this must also be kept well stopped in a bottle and wrapped in paper, as it is as apt to change as the Dutch metal.

Tin bronze.

Melt grain-tin in a ladle over the fire; when in a fluid state add by degrees quicksilver, and stir it well; it will be transformed into a greyish powder, which, for the sake of variety, you may use with others, either alone or mixed,

By mixing these different bronzes together, you may produce a great variety, that will add much to the beauty of your work; and we may here remark that there is a variety of colours in gold leaf, all of which will produce a differently-coloured powder.

In London a variety of coloured bronze can be procured at the colour shops, at less expence than we can make them; but not so in the country; we have therefore here set down those that are most generally useful.

Method of applying the bronze.

Go over the part you intend to bronze with gold size or varnish, and when it is sufficiently dry, that is, when it does not adhere to the finger, but feels clammy, dip a piece of cotton rolled hard into a ball, in your bronze powder, and dab it on the places to be bronzed.

H

To japan work-boxes, &c.

There is a very pretty method of ornamenting boxes, cabinets, &c. so that the figures appear of the colour of the wood, and the ground black; this by many is produced by first tracing out the pattern, and then pricking-in those parts which shall appear as the ground, either black or any colour at fancy. This is a very tedious process, and even when finished with the greatest care will not appear regular or well defined in the pattern. The following method will be found very expeditious, and at the same time very correct; it is but little known, and as such will to the practical japanner be the more acceptable; it may also be applied to many other purposes than here alluded to. The following preparation is necessary, and may be termed *the stopping-out mixture;* it is made by dissolving the best white bees-wax in spirits of turpentine till it is of the consistence of varnish; keep this mixture in a bottle, and when wanted for use mix sufficient for your present purpose with white lead in powder, or flake white, to give it a body, but not too thick, only so that it will flow freely from your pencil; having traced your design, go over those parts which you wish to remain of the colour of your wood, and let it dry; then mix ivory black in very fine powder with parchment or isinglass size, and go evenly and smoothly over every part of your work; it will now appear wholly black, or of whatever colour you have mixed with your size; let the whole get thoroughly dry, then with a stiffish brush, dipped in plain spirits of turpentine, rub the whole of the work well, and those parts that have been gone over with the stopping-out mixture will come off, leaving your black or other colour perfect, it will then appear as if you had pricked in your work, but much more sharp, and will, if carefully done, have a beautiful effect; you have now nothing more to do than varnish your work, as in general, and polish it as directed under the article Polishing, page 98.

In finishing your work in the manner of Indian japan, you must not be sparing of your varnish, but give it eight or ten coats, so that it will bear polishing.

Sealing-wax varnish.

For fancy work this has of late years been much used, and, if well applied, and your wax good, will be a very good imitation of Indian japan. The method of making the varnish or japan is very easy, being simply reducing the wax to a coarse powder and pouring the best spirits of wine on it in a bottle, and letting it gradually dissolve without heat, shaking the bottle occasionally till it is all dissolved. A two-ounce stick of the best wax will be enough for a quarter of a pint of spirits.

Recollect that much depends on the goodness of the sealing-wax; and that you may vary the colour of the varnish by using different coloured wax. As this varnish dries very quickly, it should not be made until it is wanted for use.

VARNISHING.

OF late years, varnishing has arrived to a state of perfection which enables the workman of the present day to finish his work in a style far superior to any thing previously known: by the help of this useful auxiliary he can heighten the beauty of fine wood, and give additional lustre to furniture; the simplicity of the process requires but little to be said on the subject, but we shall endeavour, as clearly as possible, to lay down some rules and cautions necessary to be observed, both in the making, and method of using varnish, that the work may appear as beautiful as possible.

In London it is hardly worth while to make varnish, unless in large quantities, as there are several shops where it may be had very good, and at a fair price; but in the country, where the carriage is an object, and you cannot depend upon the genuineness of the article, it is necessary to be known by the practical mechanic; yet where it can be purchased, we should recommend it to be had. The varnish generally sold for varnishing furniture, is white hard varnish.

Cautions respecting the making of varnish.

As heat in many cases is necessary to dissolve the gums used in making varnish, the best way, when practicable, is to use what the chemists call a sand bath, which is simply placing the vessel in which the varnish is, in another filled with sand, and placed on the fire; this will generally be sufficient to prevent the spirits catching fire; but in case of such accidents (which not unfrequently happens), it will be best to take a vessel sufficiently large that there shall be little danger of spilling any; indeed the vessel should never be more than two-thirds filled, but to prevent accident, have ready at hand a piece of board sufficiently large to cover the top of the vessel in case of its taking fire, as also a wet wrapper, in case it should be spilt when on fire, as water by itself thrown on it would only increase the mischief: and the person who attends the varnish-pot should have his hands covered with gloves, and if they are made of leather, and rather damp, it will effectually prevent injury. Those cautions should be well observed, or shocking personal injury may result from their neglect.

General directions in choosing gums and spirits.

In purchasing gum, examine it, and see that it consists for the most part of clear transparent lumps without a mixture of dirt; select the clearest and lightest pieces for the most particular kinds of varnish, reserving the others, when separated from extraneous matter, for the coarser varnishes. In choosing spirits of wine, the most simple test is by immersing the finger in it, and if it burns quickly out without burning the finger, it is good; but if, on the contrary, it is long in burning, and leaves any dampness remaining on the finger, it is mixed with inferior spirit; it may be also compared with other spirit, by comparing the weight of equal quantities; the lightest is the best; the goodness of spirits of turpentine may be likewise ascertained in the same manner by weighing it, and by noticing the degree of inflammability it possesses; the most inflammable is the best; and a person much in the habit of using it, will tell by the smell its good or bad qualities; for good turpentine has a pungent smell, and the bad a very disagreeable one, and not so powerful.

To varnish a piece of furniture.

First make the work quite clean; then fill up all knots or blemishes with cement of the same colour; see that your brush is clean, and free from loose hairs; then dip your brush in the varnish, stroke it along the wire raised across the top of your varnish-pot, and give the work a thin and regular coat; soon after that another, and another, always taking care not to pass the brush twice in the same place; let it stand to dry in a moderately warm place, that the varnish may not chill.

When you have given your work about six or seven coats, let it get quite hard (which you will prove by pressing your knuckles on it; if it leave a mark, it is not hard enough); then with the three first fingers of your hand rub the varnish till it chafes, and proceed over that part of the work you mean to polish, in order to take out all the streaks, or partial lumps made by the brush;

then give it another coat, and let it stand a day or two to harden.

The best vessel for holding varnish is sold at colour-shops, called a varnish pan: it is constructed of tin, with a false bottom; the interval between the two bottoms is filled with sand, which being heated over the fire, keeps the varnish fluid and flows more readily from the brush: there is a tin handle to it, and the false bottom comes sloping from one end to the other, which causes the varnish to run to one end; it has also a wire fixed across the top, to wipe the brush against.

To make the best white hard varnish.

Rectified spirits of wine, one quart; gum sandrach, ten ounces; gum mastic, two ounces; gum anime, half an ounce; dissolve these in a clean can, or bottle, in a warm place, frequently shaking it; when the gum is dissolved strain it through a lawn sieve, and it is fit for use.

To keep brushes in order.

The brushes used for varnishing are either flat in tin, or round, tied firm to the handle, and made either of camels' hair or very fine bristles; in the use of which it is necessary to be very careful in cleaning them after being used, for if laid by with the varnish in them, they are soon spoiled; therefore, after using, wash them well in spirits of wine or turpentine, according to the nature of your varnish; after which you may wash them out with hot water and soap, and they will be as good as new, and last a great while with care; and the spirits that are used for cleaning, may be used to mix with varnish for the more common purposes, or the brushes may be cleaned, merely with boiling water and strong yellow soap.

Mastic varnish for varnishing pictures or drawings.

To one pint of spirits of turpentine, put ten ounces of the cleanest gum mastic;—sit it in a sand bath till it is all dissolved, then strain it through a fine sieve, and it is ready for use; if too thick, thin it with spirits of turpentine.

Turpentine varnish.

To one pint of spirits of turpentine, add ten ounces of clear rosin pounded; put it in a tin can, on a stove, and let it boil for half an hour; when the rosin is all dissolved, let it cool, and it is fit for use.

Varnish for violins, &c.

To one pint of rectified spirits of wine, put one ounce and a half of gum mastic, and one-third of a gill of turpentine varnish; keep it in a very warm place, in a tin can, frequently shaking it, until dissolved; then strain it, and keep it for use. If it is harder than you wish, add a little more turpentine varnish.

To varnish drawings, or any kind of paper or card work.

Boil clear parchment cuttings in water in a clean

glazed pipkin, till they produce a very clear size; strain it, and keep it for use.

Give your work two coats of the above size, passing quickly over the work, not to disturb the colours; proceed as before directed (page 92,) with your varnish.

Another method still better.

Dissolve one ounce of the best isinglass in about a pint of water by simmering it over the fire; strain it through fine muslin, and keep it for use.

Try the size on a piece of paper moderately warm, and if glistens, it is too thick; add more water; if it soaks into the paper, it is too thin; add or diminish the isinglass till it merely dulls the surface; then give your drawing two or three coats, letting it dry between each being careful (particularly in the first coat) to bear very lightly on the brush (which should be a flat tin camel's hair;) the size should flow freely from it, otherwise you may damage the drawing.

Then take the best mastic varnish, and with it give at least three coats, and the effect will answer your most sanguine wishes.

This is the method used by many eminent artists, and is found superior to any that has been tried.

Amber varnish.

To eight ounces of amber in powder, add two of gum lac; melt the amber in a glazed pipkin, with half a pint of the best spirits of turpentine; and when melted, add the gum lac; place it again on the fire, and keep stirring it with a piece of wood till all is dissolved, then add one ounce of the clearest cold-drawn linseed oil; stir it well together, and strain it for use.

Oil varnish.

Boil one pint of the best linseed oil, an hour, then add a quarter of a pound of the clearest rosin in powder; stir it well till dissolved; add one ounce of spirits of turpentine; strain it and bottle for use.

This is a cheap and good varnish for sash frames, or any work where economy is required; it has, besides, the property of bearing hot water without being damaged, and is not subject to scratch.

Copal varnish.

Take spirits of wine one pint, gum copal half an ounce, and shell-lac one-fourth of an ounce; reduce the gums to powder; put the spirits in a jar or bottle, add the gums, place the whole in a warm place, with the cork lightly in the bottle; shake it occasionally, and when the gums are quite dissolved, strain and bottle for use.

To make a colourless copal varnish.

As all copal is not fit for this purpose, to ascertain such pieces as are good, each must be taken separately, and a single drop of pure essential oil of rosemary, not altered by keeping, must be let fall on it. Those pieces that soften at the part that imbibes the oil, are good; reduce them to powder, which sift through a very fine hair sieve, and put it into a glass, on the bottom of which it must not lie more than a finger's breadth thick, pour upon it essence of rosemary to a similar height; stir the whole for a few minutes, when the copal will dissolve into a viscous fluid. Let it stand for two hours, and then pour gently on it two or three drops of very pure alcohol (spirits of wine), which distribute over the oily mass by inclining the bottle in different directions with a very gentle motion; repeat this operation by little and little, till the incorporation is effected, and the varnish reduced to a proper degree of fluidity. It must then be left to stand a few days, and when clear, be decanted off. This varnish thus made without heat, may be applied with equal success to pasteboard, wood, and metals, and takes a better polish than any other; it may be used on paintings, the beauty of which it greatly heightens.

Turpentine copal varnish.

To one ounce and a half of gum copal, add eight ounces of the very best oil of turpentine; put the turpentine into a vessel, in a sand bath, when it is very hot; but be cautious not to let it boil; then gradually add the gum copal, stirring it with a wooden spatula, adding fresh gum as the other dissolves; when all is thoroughly incorporated, take the vessel off the bath and put it to cool, let it remain covered over for a few days to settle, and decant it clear off.

In making this varnish it frequently happens that the gum will not melt so readily as it ought, which, in general, is owing to the turpentine not being sufficiently rectified; but when that is good it will always succeed. It is best also to let your turpentine be exposed for some time in the sun in a corked bottle, that the watery particles may be gradually dissipated; the bottle should not be stopped quite tight.

A varnish which suits all sorts of prints and pictures, stands water, and makes the work appear as shining as glass.

Dilute one quarter of a pound of Venice turpentine, with a gill, or thereabouts, of spirit of wine; if too thick, a little more of this last; if not enough, a little more of the former, so that you bring it to the consistence of milk; lay one coat of this on the right side of the print, and when dry, it will shine like glass. If it be not to your liking, you may lay another coat on.

To make appear in gold the figures of a print.

After having laid on both sides of the print one coat of the above-described varnish, in order to make it transparent, let it dry a little while; then before it is quite so, lay some gold in leaves on the wrong side of the print, pressing it gently on with the cotton you hold in your hand. By these means all parts, whereon you shall lay these leaves, will appear like true massive gold on the right side.

When this is all thoroughly dry, lay on the right side of it, one coat of the varnish described above, and it will then be as good as any crown glass. You may also put a pasteboard behind the print to support it better in its frame.

Method of preparing the composition used for varnishing coloured drawings and prints, so as to make them resemble paintings in oil.

Take of Canada balsam one ounce, spirit of turpentine two ounces, mix them together. Before this composition is applied, the drawing or print should be sized with a solution of isinglass in water, and when dry, apply the varnish with a camel-hair brush.

POLISHING.

The beauty of Cabinet-work depends upon the care with which it is finished; some clean off with scraping and rubbing with glass-paper: this should be done in all cases, but it is not enough, particularly where the grain is anyways soft; a good glass-paper also is essential; (directions for making which will be found in our miscellaneous receipts,) a polish should then be added. But unless the varnish for cabinet-work be very clear and bright, it will give a dingy shade to all light-coloured woods; this should therefore be a previous care.

I

Again, some workmen polish with rotten stone; others with putty-powder, and others with common whiting and water; but Tripoli will be found to answer the best.

To polish varnish

Is certainly a tedious process, and considered by many as a matter of difficulty.

Put two ounces of powdered Tripoli into an earthen pot or basin, with water sufficient to cover it; then with a piece of fine flannel four times doubled, lay it over a piece of cork rubber, and proceed to polish your varnish, always wetting it with the Tripoli and water; you will know when the process is complete, by wiping a part of the work with a sponge, and observing whether there is a fair and even gloss; clean off with a bit of mutton-suet and fine flour.

Caution.—Be careful not to rub the work too hard, nor longer than is necessary to make the face perfectly smooth and even.

The French method of polishing.

With a piece of fine pumice-stone and water, pass regularly over the work with the grain, until the rising of the grain is down; then with powdered Tripoli and boiled linseed oil, polish the work to a bright face; this will be a very superior polish, but it requires considerable time.

To polish brass ornaments inlayed in wood.

The brass-work must first be filed very clean with a smooth file; then having mixed some Tripoli, powdered very fine, with linseed oil, with a rubber made from a piece of old hat, or felt, polish the work as you would polish varnish, until the desired effect is produced.

If the work be ebony, or black rose-wood, take some elder-coal powdered very fine, and apply it dry after you have done with the Tripoli; it will increase the beauty of the polish.

To polish Ivory.

If ivory be polished with putty and water, by means of a rubber made of hat, it will in a short time produce a fine gloss.

To polish any work of pearl.

Go over it with pumice stone, finely powdered (first washed to separate the impurities and dirt), with which you may polish it very smooth; then apply putty-powder as directed for ivory, and it will produce a fine gloss and a good colour.

To polish marble.

It sometimes happens that the cabinet-maker has a table-top of marble to remount, which is scratched and requires repolishing; the following is the process used by the mason, and will, therefore, be acceptable in a work like the present.—With a piece of sandstone with a very fine grit, rub your slab backwards and forwards, using very fine sand and water, till the marble appears equally rough and not in scratches; next use a finer stone and finer sand, till its surface appears equally gone over; then with fine emery powder and a piece of felt or old hat, wrapped round a weight, rub it till all the marks left by the former process are worked out, and it appears with a comparative gloss on its surface; afterwards finish the polish with putty-powder and fine clean rags; as soon as the face appears of a good gloss, do not put any more powder on your rags, but rub it well, and in a short time it will appear as fresh as when out of the mason's hands.

To polish tortoise-shell, or horn.

Having scraped your work perfectly smooth and level, rub it with very fine sand-paper or Dutch rushes; repeat the rubbing with a bit of felt dipped in very finely powdered charcoal with water, and lastly with rotten-stone or putty powder; and finish with a piece of soft wash-leather, damped with a little sweet oil.

FRICTION VARNISHING, OR FRENCH POLISHING.

The method of varnishing furniture, by means of rubbing it on the surface of the wood, is of comparatively modern date. To put on a hard face, which shall not be so liable to scratch as varnish, and yet appear equally fine, the French polish was introduced, and it would be unpardonable in a work like this, to omit a full direction of the process, and also the various preparations of the different compositions necessary.

All the polishes are used much in the same way, a general description will therefore be a sufficient guide for the workman. If your work be porous, or the grain coarse, it will be necessary, previous to polishing, to give it a coat of clear size previous to your commencing with the polish; and when dry, gently go over it with very fine glass-paper; the size will fill up the pores and prevent the waste of the polish, by being absorbed into the wood; and be also a saving of considerable time in the operation.

Make a wad with a piece of coarse flannel or drugget, by rolling it round and round, over which, on the side meant to polish with, put very fine linen rag several times doubled, to be as soft as possible; put the wad or cushion to the mouth of the bottle, containing the preparation (or polish) and shake it, which will damp the rag sufficiently, then proceed to rub your work in a circular direction, observing not to do more than about a square foot at a time; rub it lightly till the whole surface is covered; repeat this three or four times, according to the texture of the wood; each coat to be rubbed until the rag appears dry, and be careful not to put too much on the rag at a time, and you will have a very beautiful and lasting polish; be also very particular in letting your rags be very clean and soft, as the polish depends, in a great measure, on the care you take in keeping it clean and free from dust during the operation.

The true French polish.

To one pint of spirits of wine, add a quarter of an ounce of gum-copal, a quarter of an ounce of gum-arabic, and one ounce of shell-lac.

Let your gums be well bruised, and sifted through a piece of muslin, Put the spirits and the gums together in a vessel that can be close corked; place them near a warm stove, and frequently shaking them, in two or three days they will be dissolved: strain it through a piece of muslin, and keep it tight corked for use.

Another French polish.

Take one ounce each of mastic, sandarac, seed-lac, shell-lac, gum-lac, and gum-arabic; reduce them to powder, and add a quarter of an ounce of virgin-wax; put the whole into a bottle, with one quart of rectified spirit of wine; let it stand twelve hours, and it will be fit for use.

To apply it, make a ball of cloth, and put on it occasionally a little of the polish; then wrap the ball in a piece of calico, which slightly touch with linseed oil: rub the furniture hard with a circular motion, until a gloss is produced: finish in the same manner, but instead of all polish, use one-third polish to two-thirds spirits of wine.

Or, put into a glass bottle, one ounce of gum-lac, two drams of mastic in drops, four drams of sandarac, three ounces of shell-lac, and half an ounce of gum dragon; reduce the whole to powder, add to it a piece of camphor, the size of a nut, and pour on it eight ounces of rectified spirits of wine: stop the bottle close, but take care when the gums are dissolving, that it is not more than half-full; it may be placed near a gentle fire, or on a German stove; but a bath of hot sand is preferable, as avoiding all danger, the compound being so very apt to catch fire. Apply it as before.

An improved polish.

To a pint of spirits of wine, add, in fine powder, one ounce of seed-lac, two drams of gum-guaiacum, two drams of dragon's blood, and two drams of gum-mastic; expose them, in a vessel stopped close, to a moderate heat for three hours, until you find the gums dissolved; strain it into a bottle for use, with a quarter of a gill of the best linseed oil, to be shaken up well with it.

This polish is more particularly intended for dark-coloured woods, for it is apt to give a tinge to light ones, as satin-wood, or airwood, &c. owing to the admixture of the dragon's blood, which gives it a red appearance.

Water-proof polish.

Take a pint of spirits of wine, two ounces of gum-benzoin, a quarter of an ounce of gum-sandarac, and a quarter of an ounce of gum-anime; these must be put into a stopped bottle, and placed either in a sand-bath or in hot water till dissolved; then strain it; and after adding about a quarter of a gill of the best clear poppy oil, well shake it up, and put it by for use.

Bright polish.

A pint of spirits of wine to two ounces of gum-benzoin and half an ounce of gum-sandarac, put in a glass bottle corked, and placed in a sand-bath, or hot water, until you find all the gum dissolved, will make a beautiful clear polish for Tunbridge-ware goods, tea-caddies, &c.: it must be shaken from time to time, and when all dissolved, strained through a fine muslin sieve and bottled for use.

Prepared spirits.

This preparation is useful for finishing after any of the foregoing receipts, as it adds to the lustre and durability, as well as removing every defect which may happen in the other polishes; and it gives the surface a most brilliant appearance.

Half a pint of the very best rectified spirits of wine, two drams of shell-lac, and two drams of gum-benzoin. Put these ingredients in a bottle, and keep it in a warm place till the gum is all dissolved, shaking it frequently; when cold, add two tea-spoonsful of the best clear white poppy oil; shake them well together, and it is fit for use.

This preparation is used in the same manner as foregoing polishes, but, in order to remove all dull places, you may increase the pressure in rubbing.

Strong polish,

To be used in the carved parts of cabinet work with a brush, as in standards, pillars, claws, &c.

Dissolve two ounces of seed-lac and two ounces of white rosin in one pint of spirits of wine.

This varnish or polish must be laid on warm, and if the work can be warmed also, it will be so much the better; at any rate moisture and dampness must be avoided.

Directions for cleaning and polishing old furniture.

Take a quart of stale beer or vinegar, put a handful of common salt, and a table-spoonful of spirits of salt into it, and boil it for a quarter of an hour; you may keep it in a bottle, and warm it when wanted for use; having previously washed your furniture with soft hot water to get the dirt off, wash it carefully with the above mixture; then polish, according to the directions, with any of the foregoing polishes.

PART V.

GLUES, CEMENTS, &c.

CEMENTS.

To make mahogany-coloured cement.

MELT two ounces of bees' wax, and half an ounce
of rosin together; then add half an ounce of Indian
red, and a small quantity of yellow ochre, to bring it
to the desired colour: keep it in a pipkin for use.

Portable glue, or bank-note cement.

Boil one pound of the best glue, strain it very clear;
boil also four ounces of isinglass; put it into a double
glue-pot, with half a pound of fine brown sugar, and
boil it pretty thick; then pour it into plates or moulds.
when cold, you may cut and dry them for the pocket.

This glue is very useful to draftsmen, architects, &c.
as it immediately dilutes in warm water, and fastens
the paper without the process of damping: or it may

be used by softening it in the mouth, and applying it
to the paper.

Cement for turners.

Melt together bees'-wax one ounce, rosin half an
ounce, and pitch half an ounce; stir in it some very
fine brick-dust to give it a body; if too soft, add more
rosin; if too hard, more wax: when nearly cold, make
it up into cakes or rolls, which keep for use.

This will be found very useful for fastening any piece
of wood on your chuck, which is done by applying
your roller of cement to the chuck, while going round;
it will melt the cement; then apply the piece of wood
you wish to affix to the chuck, and it will adhere with
sufficient force.

A cement for broken glass.

Steep one ounce of isinglass in half a pint of spirits
of wine, for twenty-four hours, then let it dissolve over
a slow fire (always keeping it covered, or the spirit will
evaporate); now well bruise six cloves of garlic in a
mortar, put them in a linen cloth, and squeeze the juice
into the isinglass, mix all well together and keep it for
use. It is excellent to join glass ornaments, &c.

A cement to stop flaws or cracks in wood, of any colour.

Put any quantity of fine saw-dust of the same wood
your work is made with, into an earthen-pan, and pour
boiling water on it, stir it well, and let it remain for a

week or ten days, occasionally stirring it; then boil it for some time, and it will be of the consistence of pulp or paste; put it into a coarse cloth, and squeeze all the moisture from it; keep it for use, and when wanted, mix a sufficient quantity of thin glue to make it a paste; rub it well into the cracks, or fill up the holes in your work with it; when quite hard and dry, clean your work off, and if carefully done, you will scarcely discern the imperfection.

A cement for joining china, &c.

Beat the whites of eggs well to a froth, let them settle, add soft grated or sliced cheese and quicklime; beat them well together, and apply a little to the broken edges; it will endure both the heat of the fire and water.

Another cement.*

Pound half an ounce of rosin and four ounces of gum-mastic, put them into a pipkin on the fire to melt; stir them well; to this add about half an ounce of finely-powdered glass, and half an ounce of quicklime; stir the whole well together; when nearly cold, form it into sticks, on a stone, in the same manner as sticks of sealing-wax are formed; when you want to cement any article, heat the broken edges sufficiently to melt your cement, which rub thinly on both edges; bring them accurately together; press them close, and let them cool; which, if carefully done, your work will sooner break in any other part than where the cement has been applied.

A strong glue that will resist moisture.

Dissolve gum-sandarac and mastic, of each a quarter of an ounce, in a quarter of a pint of spirits of wine, to which add a quarter of an ounce of clear turpentine; now take strong glue, or that in which isinglass has been dissolved; then putting the gums into a double glue-pot, add by degrees the glue, constantly stirring it over the fire till the whole is well incorporated; strain it through a cloth, and it is ready for use; you may now return it into the glue-pot, and add half an ounce of very finely powdered glass; use it quite hot. If you join two pieces of wood together with it, you may, when perfectly hard and dry, immerse it in water, and the joint will not separate.

Another glue for the same purpose.

To two quarts of skimmed milk add half a pound of the best glue: melt them together, taking care they do not boil over, and you will have a very strong glue which will resist damp or moisture.

To make paste for laying the cloth or leather on table-tops.

To a pint of the best wheaten flour add rosin, very finely powdered, about two large spoonfuls; of alum one spoonful in powder; mix them all well together, put them into a pan, and add by degrees soft or rain water, carefully stirring it till it is of the consistence of thinnish cream, put it into a sauce-pan over a clear

K

fire, keeping it constantly stirred that it may not get lumpy; when it is of a stiff consistence, so that the spoon will stand upright in it, it is done enough; be careful to stir it well from the bottom, for it will burn if not well attended to; empty it out into a pan, and cover it over till cold to prevent a skin forming on the top, which would make it lumpy.

This paste is very superior for the purpose, and adhesive. To use it for cloth or baize, spread the paste evenly and smoothly, on the top of the table, and lay your cloth on it, pressing and smoothing it with a flat piece of wood; let it remain till dry, then trim the edges close to the cross-banding; if you cut it close at first, it will in drying shrink and look bad where it meets the banding all round. If used for leather, the leather must be first previously damped, and then the paste spread over it; then lay it on the table, and rub it smooth and level with a linen cloth, and cut the edges close to the banding, with a short knife. Some lay their table cover with glue instead of paste, and perhaps, for cloth, it is the best method, but for leather it is not proper, as glue is apt to run through; in using it for cloth great care must be taken that your glue is not too thin, and that you rub the cloth well down with a thick piece of wood made hot at the fire, for the glue soon chills; you may in this method cut off the edges close to the border at once.

MISCELLANEOUS RECEIPTS.

Glass paper.

TAKE any quantity of broken window-glass; that which has rather a green appearance on the edge, is best; pound it in an iron mortar, then have two or three sieves of different degrees of fineness, ready for use when wanted; take any good tough paper, (fine cartridge is the best,) level the nobs and bumps from both sides with pumice-stone; tack it at each corner on a board, and with good clear glue, diluted with about one-third more water than is used generally for wood-work, go quickly over the paper, taking care to spread it even with your brush; then, having your sieve ready, sift the pounded glass over it lightly, but to cover it in every part; let it remain till the glue is set, take it from the board, shake off the superfluous glass into the sieve, and hang it in the shade to dry: in two or three days it will be fit for use.

This paper will be much better than any you can buy, sand being frequently mixed with the glass, and coloured to deceive the purchaser.

To clean the face of soft mahogany, or other porous wood.

After scraping and sand-papering in the usual manner, take a sponge and well wet the surface to raise the grain; then with a piece of fine pumice-stone, free from stony particles, and cut the way of the fibres, rub the wood in the direction of the grain, keeping it moist with water: let the work dry, then if you wet it again, you will find the grain much smoother, and it will not raise so much; repeat the process, and you will find the surface perfectly smooth, and the texture of the wood much hardened: by this means, common soft Honduras mahogany will have a face equal to fine Hispaniola.

If this does not succeed to your satisfaction, you may improve the surface, by using the pumice-stone with cold drawn linseed oil, in the same manner as you proceeded with water; this will be found to put a most beautiful, as well as a durable face to your work, which may then be polished or varnished.

Another way to clean and finish mahogany work.

Scrape and sand-paper your work as smooth as possible, go over every part with a brush dipped in furniture oil, and let it remain all night; have ready the powder of the finest red brick, which tie up in a cotton stocking and sift it equally over the work the next morning, and with a leaden or iron weight in a piece of carpet, rub your work well the way of the grain backwards and forwards till it has a good gloss; if not sufficient, or if the grain appears any way rough, repeat the process; be careful not to put too much of the brick dust, as it should not be rubbed dry, but rather as a paste upon the cloth; when the surface is perfectly smooth, clean your work off with a rubber of carpet, and fine mahogany sawdust. This process will give a good gloss and face to your work, and make a surface that will improve by wear; indeed, by this process, soft Honduras mahogany will have the appearance of Spanish.

To darken light mahogany.

In repairing old furniture, it frequently happens that we cannot match the old wood; therefore, after the repairs are completed, to prevent the pieces introduced looking like patches, wash them with soap-lees, or dissolve quick-lime in water, and use in the same manner; but be careful not to let either be too strong, or it will make the wood too dark; it is best, therefore, to use it rather weak at first, and if not dark enough, repeat the process till the wood is sufficiently darkened.

To cut good steel scrapers.

Part of the blade of a broken saw makes the best scrapers; but as it is hard, it is very difficult to cut it in the required form; the best and most expeditious way is to mark it out to the size wanted, and then to place the blade or steel plate in a vice whose chaps shut very close, placing the mark even with the face of the vice, and the part to be cut to waste above the vice, then with a cold chisel or a common steel firmer that has its basil broken off, holding it close to the vice and rather inclined upwards, begin at one end of the steel plate, and with a sharp blow of the hammer it will cut it; keep going on by degrees, and you will with ease cut it to the shape required; then grind the edges of your scraper level, and finish by rubbing it on your Turkey-stone.

To sharpen and set a saw.

First run a file along the edge of the teeth till you see them range in a direct line, then lay the blade on a smooth piece of lead, or on the end of your trying-plane, and with a square steel punch give a gentle tap on it with a hammer, after placing it on one of the teeth, do the same with every alternate tooth; reverse the saw and punch the teeth on the other side, and look down your saw that the teeth are all equally set, then begin with your file at that part of your saw nearest the handle; to sharpen or file the teeth to a good point, hold your file so that it makes an angle, with the saw-blade, of about thirty degrees, or two-thirds that of a mitre angle, observing to shift the file for every alternate tooth in an opposite inclination, and bringing each tooth to a very sharp point; and keep the upper edge of your file very nearly horizontal; every tooth will then represent a sharp chisel, and cut as it goes, without tearing.

To take bruises out of furniture.

Wet the part with warm water; double a piece of brown paper five or six times, soak it, and lay it on the place; apply on that a hot flat-iron till the moisture is evaporated; if the bruise be not gone, repeat the process. After two or three applications, the dent or bruise will be raised level with the surface. If the bruise be small, merely soak it with warm water, and apply a red-hot poker very near the surface; keep it continually wet, and in a few minutes the bruise will disappear.

To make anti-attrition.

According to the specification of the patent, this mixture is made of one part of plumbago or black-lead ground very fine, and four parts of hogs-lard or other grease mixed well together. It prevents the effects of friction, much better than oil or other grease, and is very useful to the turner, and will be found to make the lathe work much easier, as well as be a great saving in oil, which with constant use grows stiff, and sensibly impedes the motion; while this preparation once applied will last a long time without requiring renewal.

Polish for turner's work.

Dissolve sandarac in spirits of wine, in the proportion of one ounce of sandarac to half a pint of spirits, next shave bees'-wax one ounce, and dissolve it in a sufficient quantity of spirits of turpentine to make it into a paste; add the former mixture by degrees to it, then with a woollen cloth, apply it to the work while it is in motion in the lathe, and with a soft linen rag polish it; it will appear as if highly varnished.

To clean and restore the elasticity of cane chair bottoms, couches, &c.

Turn up the chair bottom, and with hot water and a sponge, wash the cane-work, so that it may be thoroughly soaked; should it be dirty, use a little soap; let it dry in the air, and it will be as tight and firm as when new, provided the cane be not broken.

To clean silver furniture.

Lay the furniture, piece by piece, upon a charcoal fire, and when they are just red, take them off and boil them in tartar and water, and your silver will have the same beauty as when first made.

To clean marble, sienna, jasper, porphyry, or scagliola.

Mix the strongest soap-lees with quick-lime, to the consistency of milk, lay it on the stone, &c. for twenty-four hours; then clean it off, and wash with soap and water, and it will appear as new.

This may be improved by rubbing or polishing it afterwards with fine putty-powder and olive oil.

To take ink-spots out of mahogany.

Apply spirits of salts with a rag, until the spots disappear, and immediately afterwards wash with clear water.

Another method.

To half a pint of soft water, put an ounce of oxalic-

—To take ink stains from paper: Make a solution of muriate of tin, two drachms; water, four drachms. Apply with a camel's hair brush. After the stain has disappeared the paper should be passed through water and dried.

acid, and half an ounce of butter of antimony; shake it well, and when dissolved it will be very useful in extracting stains out of mahogany, as well as ink, if not of too long standing.

To make furniture paste.

Scrape two ounces of bees'-wax into a pot or basin; then add as much spirits of turpentine as will moisten it through; at the same time powder an eighth part of an ounce of rosin, and add to it, when dissolved to the consistence of paste, as much Indian red as will bring it to a deep mahogany colour: stir it up, and it will be fit for use.

Another method.

Scrape two ounces of bees'-wax as before, then to half a pint of spirits of turpentine in a clean glazed pipkin, add half an ounce of alkanet root; cover it close, and put it over a slow fire, attending it carefully, that it may not boil, or catch fire; when you perceive the colour to be drawn from the root, by the liquid being of a deep red, add as much of it to the wax as will moisten it through; at the same time add the eighth part of an ounce of powdered rosin, cover it close, and let it stand six hours, and it will be fit for use.

To make furniture oil.

Put linseed-oil in a glazed pipkin, with as much alkanet-root as it will cover; let it boil gently, till it

becomes of a strong red colour; let it cool, and it will
be fit for use.

Another method.

Boil together cold-drawn linseed-oil and as much
alkanet-root as it will cover, and to every pint of oil
add one ounce of the best rose pink; when all the
colour is extracted, strain it off, and to every pint add
half a gill of spirits of turpentine: and it will be a
very superior composition for soft and light mahogany.

Black wax

Is made of one ounce of bees'-wax to half an ounce
of Burgandy pitch; melt them together, and add one
ounce and a half of ivory-black, ground very fine and
dried.

Green Wax.

Melt one ounce of bees'-wax, and add half an ounce
of verditer; let the pipkin be large enough, as it will
immediately boil up; stir it well, and add the eighth
part of an ounce of rosin; it will be sufficiently hard,
and fit for use.

To take out spots of oil or grease from cloth.

Drop on the spot some oil of tartar or salt of worm-
wood, which has been left in a damp place till it turns
into a fluid; then immediately wash the place with
luke-warm soft water, and then with cold water, and
the spot will disappear.

This will be found very useful, as it frequently happens that the cloth of card tables, and the inside flaps of secretaries, are spotted and greasy, which by proceeding as above will completely take out every spot of grease.

To take out wax spots from cloth or silk.

Put on each spot a piece of soft soap, and place it in the sun, or gently warm it before the fire; let it remain some time, then wash it off with soft water, and the spot will have disappeared.

Another method.

Drop spirits of turpentine or spirits of wine on the spot; then with a sponge rub it gently; repeat it till the spot disappears.

To make parchment transparent.

Soak a thin skin of parchment in a strong lye of wood-ashes, often wringing it out till you find it becomes transparent, then strain it on a frame and let it dry.

This will be much improved, if after it is dry you give it a coat, on both sides, of clear mastic varnish diluted with spirits of turpentine.

To soften ivory.

Slice a quarter of a pound of mandrake, and put it in half a pint of the best vinegar, into which put your ivory; let it stand in a warm place for forty-eight hours, you will then be able to bend the ivory to your mind.

To bleach ivory.

Take a double handful of lime, and slack it by sprinkling it with water, then add three pints of water, and stir it up together; let it settle ten minutes, and pour the water into a pan for your purpose; then take your ivory, and steep it in the lime-water, twenty-four hours, after which boil it in strong alum-water one hour, and dry it in the air.

To solder or weld tortoise-shell or horn.

Provide yourself with a pair of pincers or tongs, so constructed that you can reach four inches beyond the rivet; then have your tortoise-shell filed clean to a lap-joint, carefully observing that there is no grease about it, wet the joint with water; apply the pincers hot, following them with water, and you will find the shell to be joined as it were one piece.

To clean carpets or tapestry.

Your carpet being first well beat, and freed from dust, tack it down to the floor; then mix half a pint of bullock's gall with two gallons of soft water; scrub it well with soap and this gall mixture; let it remain till quite dry, and it will be perfectly cleansed, and look like new, as the colours will be restored to their original brightness; the brush you use must not be too hard, but rather long in the hair, or you will rub up the nap, and damage the article.

To make composition ornaments for picture frames, or other purposes.

Mix as much whiting as you think you shall have occasion for, for present use, with thinnish glue to the consistence of putty, and having a mould ready, rub it well all over with sweet oil, and press your composition in it; take it out, and you will have a good impression, which you may set by to dry; or if wanted, you may, before it gets hard, apply it to your work with thick glue, and bend it into the form required.

If you have not a mould at hand, you may make one of the composition from any leaf or pattern you may wish to copy, and letting it get hard, use it as a mould, first oiling it well.

You will find this composition of great use for copying any pattern from good moulds.

To clean pictures.

Having taken the picture out of its frame, take a clean towel, and making it quite wet, lay it on the face of your picture, sprinkling it from time to time with clean soft water; let it remain wet for two or three days, take the cloth off and renew it with a fresh one; after wiping your picture with a clean wet sponge, repeat the process till you find all the dirt soaked out of your picture; then wash it with a soft sponge, and

let it get quite dry; rub it with some clear nut or linseed oil, and it will look as well as when fresh done.

Another method.

Put into two quarts of strong lye a quarter of a
pound of Genoa soap, rasped very fine, with a pint of
spirits of wine; let them simmer on the fire for half an
hour, then strain them through a cloth, apply it with a
brush to the picture, wipe it off with a sponge, and
apply it a second time, which will remove all dirt; then
with a little nut-oil, warmed, rub the picture and let it
dry; this will make it look as bright as when it came
out of the artist's hand.

To silver clock faces, the scales of barometers, &c.

Take half an ounce of old silver lace, add an ounce
of the best nitric acid, put them in an earthen pot and
place them over a gentle fire till all is dissolved, which
will happen in about five minutes; then take them off
and mix it in a pint of clear water, after which pour it
into another vessel, and free it from sediment; then add
a spoonful of common salt, and the silver will be pre-
cipitated in the form of a white powder or curd; pour
off the acid, and mix the curd with two ounces of salt
of tartar, half an ounce of whiting, and a large spoonful of salt; mix it up together, and it is ready for use.

In order to apply the above composition, clean your
brass or copper plate with some rotten stone and a
piece of old hat; rub it with salt and water with your

hand; then take a little of the composition on your finger, and rub it over your plate, and it will firmly adhere and completely silver it; wash it well with water; when dry, rub it with a clean rag, and varnish it.

This silver is not durable, but may be improved by heating the article and repeating the operation till the covering seems thick enough, or by varnishing it in the following manner.

Varnish for clock faces, &c.

Take of spirits of wine one pint, divide it into four parts; mix one part with half an ounce of gum mastic, in a bottle by itself; one part of spirits, and half an ounce of gum sandarac in another bottle; and one part of spirits and half an ounce of the whitest part of gum benjamin, mix and temper them to your mind; if too thick, add spirits; if too thin, some mastic; if too soft, some sandarac or benjamin when you use it, warm the silvered plate before the fire, and with a flat camel-hair pencil, stroke it over till no white streaks appear, and this will preserve the silvering for many years.

Crystallized tin.

Take sheet tin, the best, and thickest covered with the metal you can get, clean it well with whiting and water till the face is well polished; warm it, or lay it on a hot plate, and with a sponge or brush wet it well with strong spirits of salts; you will soon see it shoot into beautiful patterns; as soon as this happens, plunge it into cold spring water; you may then varnish it with any colour you please, or leave it in its natural state and varnish with clear varnish.

This has of late been much introduced into furniture, and when well executed has a beautiful appearance; you may use it as a veneer in the manner of buhl work, having first given the side you intend to be glued to your work a good coat of paint.

To render plaster figures very durable.

Set the figure in a warm place to get thoroughly dry; then have a vessel large enough to contain it, which fill so that when the plaister figure is placed in it, it will be quite covered with the best and clearest linseed oil just warm; let it remain in the vessel for twelve or fourteen hours; then take it out, let it drain, and set it in a place free from dust; and when the oil is quite dry, the ornament, or whatever is thus prepared, will look like wax, and will bear washing without injury.

To make transparent, or tracing paper.

Dissolve a piece of white bees'-wax, about the size of a walnut, in half a pint of spirits of turpentine; then having procured some very fine white wove tissue paper, lay it on a clean board, and with a soft brush dipped in this liquid, go over it on one side, and then turn it over, and apply it to the other; hang it up in a place free from dust, to dry; it will be ready for use in a few days; some add a small quantity of resin, or use resin instead of wax.

This will be found very useful to the workmen for copying any ornaments or figures, as by merely laying it on the work, you can trace every line with a pencil, and if you please, copy it correctly on fair paper, at your leisure; or if it is a pattern for Buhl-work, you may paste your tracing paper on the work you wish to cut, and follow your pattern, as directed under the article Buhl-work; it will be also found very handy for copying sketches or drawings.

To gild metal by dissolving gold in aqua regia.

Dissolve gold in aqua regia, and into the solution dip linen rags; take them out and dry them gently; then burn them to tinder; after you have well polished your work with this, take a cork and dipping it into common salt and water, and afterwards into the tinder, rub your work well, and its surface will be gilt.

Aqua regia is compounded of two parts of nitrous acid (aqua fortis) and one part of muriatic acid (spirits of salt) mixed together.

To silver ivory.

Pound a small piece of nitrate of silver (lunar caustic) in a mortar, add soft water to it, and mix them well together; keep it in a phial for use; when you wish to silver any ivory article, immerse it in this solution, and let it remain till it turns of a deep yellow,

then place it in clear water, and expose it to the rays
of the sun; or if you wish to depicture a figure or
cypher on your ivory, dip a camel-hair pencil in the
solution, and draw the subject on the ivory; after it
has turned a deep yellow, wash it well with water, and
place it in the sun-shine, occasionally wetting it with
pure water; in a short time it will turn of a black
colour, which if well rubbed will change to a brilliant
silver.

To clean mirrors, looking-glasses, &c.

Take a soft sponge, wash it well in clean water,
and squeeze it as dry as possible; dip it into some
spirits of wine, and rub over the glass, then have some
powder-blue tied up in a rag, and dust it over your
glass, rub it lightly and quickly with a soft cloth, afterwards finish with a silk handkerchief.

To clean or-moulu ornaments.

When the expence of regilding these ornaments is an
object, the following method will in a great measure
restore them to their original beauty; but if very much
worn the only way is to take off what remains of the
original gilding, and clean them well, by immersing
them in aqua-regia, or a mixture of muriatic acid and
aqua-fortis, and repeating the original process, which
is similar to that of gilding buttons; however, if not
in a very bad state, let your ornaments lay some little
time in a weakish mixture of aqua-fortis, and then

wash them directly in water; lay them on your hot plate, and when sufficiently heated apply very pale gold lacker, and they will look very well, as what remains of the original gilding will not be injured by the aqua-fortis, though the other parts as well as the gold will be perfectly cleansed from every dirt or tarnish.

A green paint for garden stands, venetian blinds, tre-lisses, &c.

Take mineral green, and white lead ground in tur-pentine, mix up the quantity you wish with a small quantity of turpentine-varnish; this serves for the first coat; for the second, put as much varnish in your mixture as will produce a good gloss; if you desire a brighter green, add a small quantity of Prussian blue, which will much improve the beauty of the colour.

To preserve wood against injury from fire.

Put into a pot an equal quantity of finely pulverised iron filings, brickdust, and ashes; pour over them glue water or size; set the whole near the fire, and when warm, stir them well together. With this liquid wash over all the wood work which might be in danger; and, on its getting dry, give it a second coat, when it will be proof against damage by fire.

To remove stains in tables.

Wash the surface over with stale beer or vinegar, and the stains will then be removed by rubbing them with a rag dipped in spirits of salts; to repolish, proceed as you would do with new work.

If the work be not stained, wash the surface with clean spirits of turpentine, and repolish it with furniture oil.

Hints in making and using glue.

The hotter glue is, the more force it will exert in keeping the two parts glued together; therefore, in all large and long joints, the glue should be applied immediately after boiling. Glue loses much of its strength by being often melted, that glue, therefore, which is newly made, is much preferable to that which has been used.

To renew a polished surface.

When furniture has been finished with wax composition, the polish may be renewed by repeating the original process of the wax composition with a small quantity carefully rubbed off.

To clean off the surface of solid work.

First smooth it with a finely-set smoothing-plane, and reduce the ridges by a scraper; then rub the surface with glass paper, finishing it with the finest kind: but if the wood be of an open grain, you must, in addition to the above, wet the surface uniformly with a wet sponge, and when it is dry, rub it a second time with glass-paper, till sufficiently smooth.

Or,

While the surface is wet, rub it with pumice-stone, in the direction of the fibres; and when it is dry, wet it again, and the grain will be raised in a less degree than by the first wetting; the rubbing being now repeated, the surface will be found to be still more compact, and susceptible of a much finer polish.

To clean lackered work in brass furniture.

If the stain or blemish be not too deeply seated, washing it with a soft linen or muslin rag wetted with warm water, will remove it: If this does not succeed, you have no resource but to re-lacker.

To cast ornaments or moulding to resemble wood.

Make a very clear cement of five parts of Flanders glue, and one part of isinglass, by dissolving the two kinds separately in a large quantity of water; then, after having separated those parts which could not be dissolved, by straining them through fine linen, mix them together. The glue thus prepared must be so much heated, that the finger can but only endure the temperature; by this a little water is evaporated, and thus the glue acquires more consistence. Mix raspings of wood, or saw-dust, passed through a fine sieve, with the glue, forming it into a paste. Having rubbed the plaister or sulphur mould with linseed or nut oil, as in plaister casts, put in the paste, and press the parts by

hand, so that no vacuity may remain; and in order
that the whole may acquire a perfect form, cover it
with an oiled board, and place a weight on it; when
the cast is dry, remove the rough parts; and if any
inequalities remain, they are to be smoothed. The
ornament thus prepared may be fixed with glue to the
article intended.

To clean a veneered surface.

Having scraped away the glue, tooth the surface in
an oblique direction to the fibres, and in proportion as
the surface acquires regularity, set the plane finer.
The final part of the operation of planing is accom-
plished by a fine-tooth plane. Remove the marks of
the tooth-plane by a scraper, and finish the surface
with glass-paper, or with pumice-stone and glass-paper.
Veneers being of a closer texture than solid wood
generally is, do not require so much labour as open-
grained solid wood.

Grease or dirt in French polish

May be readily removed by rubbing it quickly over
with a little spirit of turpentine; and which, if carefully done, will not soften the varnish.

Cement stopping.

Mix equal quantities of saw-dust of the same wood
required to be stopped, and clear glue; and with this
stop up the holes or defects of the wood; but where

the surface is to be japanned or painted, whiting may be used instead of saw-dust. Be sure to let the stopping dry before you attempt to finish the surface.

Directions in the choice of tools.

With respect to choosing the tools used in the cabinet trade, the most necessary are planes, saws, and chisels; we will consider them first with respect to the wood they are manufactured from; and secondly the steel which forms the cutting part of them: Beech is in general, and ought to be always, used for the purpose of the stocks, handles, &c., as it is of a tough texture, and not liable to split or warp so much as any other; now there are two kinds of beech, usually known by the names of black or red beech, and the white beech; the former is by far the best in every respect, and may be always known by its colour, and texture, which is darker and more hard in substance; the white is also more apt to warp, and soon wears with use; it should therefore always be rejected as improper; again, if you examine a piece of beech endways, you will perceive the grain runs in streaks, which among workmen, is called the *beat* of the wood; and in all planes this grain or beat, which is the hard fibrous particles of the wood, should run in a direction perpendicular to the face of the plane, which in that case appears full of little hard specks; whereas, if the beat runs parallel to the face, it will appear in irregular streaks, which situation of the grain should always be

avoided, as the face will be apt to wear uneven, and
more subject to warp and twist: again, in saw handles,
and stocks for bits, the beat should run in the same
direction as the saw blade, or in the same direction as
the stock, when laid on its side. In moulding planes
it is very frequently the case, that pieces of box are
let into that part of the face that forms the quirk
of the mouldings; but that, when possible, should be
avoided, as the texture of the two woods are very
different, and the different temperature of the atmosphere will cause a difference in their contraction, and
consequently the plane will be liable to cast: if it is
at any time necessary, introduce a small piece just at
the mouth of the plane, firmly dove-tailed in, which
will not be so apt to derange the accuracy of the plane.

The temper of saws, chisels, and other edge tools.

The quality of the steel should be uniform throughout; indeed, it is always better to have them tempered rather too hard than soft, for use will reduce the
temperature. If at any time it is necessary to perform the operation yourself, the best method is, to melt
a sufficient quantity of lead to immerse the cutting
part of the tool in. Having previously brightened its
surface, plunge it into the melted lead for a few minutes, till it gets sufficiently hot to melt a candle, with
which rub its surface, then plunge it in again, and
keep it there till the steel assumes a straw colour, but
be careful not to let it turn blue; when that is the

case, take it out, rub it again with the tallow, and let it cool: if it should be too soft, wipe the grease off, and repeat the process without the tallow, and when it is sufficiently hot, plunge it into cold spring water, or water and vinegar mixed. By a proper attention to these directions, and a little practice, every workman will have it in his power to give a proper temper to the tools he may use: if a saw is too hard, it may be tempered by the same means, but as it would be not only expensive, but, in many cases, impossible to do it at home, a plumber's shop is mostly at hand, where you may repeat the process when they are melting a pot of lead; but here, observe that the temper necessary is different to other cutting tools: you must wait till the steel just begins to turn blue, which is a temper that will give it more elasticity, and at the same time sufficient hardness.

FINIS.

M

INDEX.

INDEX.

INDEX.

INDEX.

INDEX.

INDEX

INDEX.

INDEX.

INDEX.

INDEX.

INDEX.

Dean and Munday, Printers, Threadneedle-Street.

CPSIA information can be obtained at www.ICGtesting.com
Printed in the USA
BVOW11*1201130315

390970BV00013B/1/P